Developmental Dyspraxia

by

Madeleine M. Portwood,
Specialist Senior Educational Psychologist

Illustrations
John O'Neill

Educational Psychology Service,
County Hall,
Durham DL1 5UJ

Published by Durham County Council

$\mathcal{A}$cknowledgements

I would like to thank the children, parents and professional colleagues who have provided the information discussed in this manual.

In particular I have benefited from the support of the Educational Psychologists in the Durham Service and the Director of Education, Keith Mitchell. Contributions made by Lorna Tones and Andrea Emerson, Special Educational Needs Support Service, who carried out and adapted many of my programmes, and Jeanne Rutter, reception class teacher, Peases West Primary School, who provided additional material, have been invaluable.

In addition I thank Christine Thurmer, Special Educational Needs Co-ordinator, Plawsworth Road Infants School, and Sue Coward, Special Educational Needs Co-ordinator, Hermitage Comprehensive School, Chester-le-Street, who committed a great deal of time, energy and patience to in-school projects.

Finally, I thank those directly involved with the production of this material:

John O'Neill for his inspired illustrations
Len Davies for his examination of content
Peter Chislett for his rigorous editing
Maureen Davison and Julie Marie Bailey, who managed
to type my often indecipherable handwritten notes.

Copyright © 1996 Madeleine Portwood.

Published by: Durham County Council,
                             County Hall,
                             Durham.
                             DH1 5UJ.

ISBN 1 897585 21 7

Contents

oreword

Dyspraxia is a condition upon which there are many differing views. Definitions have often been confusing or incomprehensible to both parents and professionals alike and the subject always raises more questions than there are answers.

In this book Madeleine Portwood, in her position as Specialist Senior Educational Psychologist, imparts her experience of working with a large cross-section of children of all ages with a varying degree of learning difficulty. The children invariably exhibit behavioural problems as well as immaturity in language, handwriting and social skills. In the past many professionals have produced studies or theories about the causes of, and remediation programmes for, dyspraxia. Whilst all have in some way contributed to better understanding of the condition there have been few attempts to combine a useful reference book for both the PROFESSIONAL and PARENT.

For the <u>parent</u> it contains a wealth of practical tips to assist with dressing, feeding, sleeping, toilet-training and developing of relationships with the child's peer group. There are also numerous interesting and lively games to help improve fine motor skills and hand-eye co-ordination, as well as sound advice on ways of making the dyspraxic child's school and home life easier. The programmes are similarly of benefit to children of secondary school age.

Equally, for <u>professionals</u> involved in education there are a number of individual remediation programmes for all ages of child together with appropriate case studies.

Finally, this book should prove to be an invaluable resource to all those involved in the development and education of dyspraxic children. Early recognition of the condition is essential in order that this 'hidden handicap' can be addressed, the difficulties understood by all and, most importantly, self-esteem restored to those who suffer.

Richard Hollick
Chairman
Dyspraxia Trust

*reface*

"*Clumsy*" is a miserable label to live with, and "clumsy kids" suffer from an accumulating social handicap throughout their schooldays, whose likely toll later has not even been estimated in terms of their adult disadvantage and despair. Disappointment, even humiliation, associated with everyday drawing, writing, gym or team sports can be compounded if attentional disorder, language problems or learning difficulties are also associated with *Developmental Dyspraxia*, and in our experience a constellation of problems is often associated with more severe cases of dyspraxia.

It is these severely affected children, probably first noticed by Health Visiting checks and then assessed systematically during screening by the School Medical Service, who are likely to benefit from this book. Those who care for them, in the family, the school or the clinic, should find it a spur to developing better and better practice for their *effective* rehabilitation.

Past practices left a great deal to be desired. A "clinical audit" by Community Paediatricians established a need to improve the recognition, referral and treatment of dyspraxia. Above all, there was a need for a better understanding of the condition, among Health Service and Education professionals and parents struggling with a maze of contradictory advice or changing fashions in treatment.

These concerns were not restricted to Cambridge. When I submitted a short note on dyspraxia to the journal *Physiotherapy* in 1994, I was astonished by the subsequent flood of mail from professionals all over the world. Most of this was along the lines of: *Are you really seeing children like ours? What works? How soon can you let us know?* In 1995 the Child Development Centre presented a very preliminary picture of our randomised controlled trial of treatment, at an Anglia and Oxford Regional Health Authority conference. There was "standing room only". We were also able to study patterns of handwriting, thanks to a small grant from the Nuffield Foundation for a Psychology student project. Well, when it came time to outline this project at a Regional dyspraxia study day, we had to turn people away who wanted to squeeze into that session. It is beginning to look as though we would need to book Wembley Stadium if we ever had any conclusive findings to present to all the clinicians with an interest in dyspraxia!

None the less, the good news is already beginning to emerge, in the following Chapters based on extensive practical experience in Durham. Children with severe dyspraxia have specific needs. In observable, measurable ways, they do respond to specific treatments. "Clumsiness" is not an indelible label.

Dr. Woody Caan
Head of Research and Development
Lifespan Healthcare, Cambridge.
A Cambridge University Teaching Trust

April, 1996

Developmental Dyspraxia

Chapter

1

Introduction

*T*his manual is the product of a desire to understand the term **dyspraxia**, in the face of numerous and often conflicting definitions, and is the result of six years' research into the subject.

In 1988 when I held Durham Local Education Authority's post as Specialist Senior Educational Psychologist for children with emotional and behavioural difficulties, I attended a seminar to discuss the increasing number of research papers suggesting that pupils exhibiting such problems were likely to have varying degrees of neurological immaturity.

Initially, it was important to determine locally whether this was indeed the case. I decided to screen youngsters in the county aged between 9 and 16 who had been identified as having special educational needs and allocated day or residential provision for their behavioural difficulties. I discovered that 82 (77%) in the sample of 107 pupils exhibited symptoms of neurological immaturity. As the proportion was so high it could be assumed that this factor must have played a significant part in the development of subsequent unacceptable behaviours.

As expected, the case histories of these pupils showed failure in school from a very early age, but the 'pure' assessment information was clouded by additional problems in the social background of many of the cases. Some had suffered extensive emotional and material deprivation, others had presented from a very early age as extremely difficult youngsters with parents seeking respite care and/or medication to enable them to cope.

Consequently, assumptions are frequently made when attempting to determine a 'cause' for these behaviours; too much emphasis can be placed on environmental and social factors instead of exploring factors within the child.

A sample of 12 pupils was selected from the identified 82, whose intellectual ability assessed using the Wechsler Intelligence Scale for Children -RS was in the average range despite a number of very low scores in some of the sub-tests. In addition these youngsters had spelling ages of at least 3 years below their chronological age and their handwriting ranged from barely legible to illegible. In the sample 9 had reading ages assessed using the Edwards Test which were above their chronological age.

Individual motor skills programmes were provided for each child and were followed daily for 20 minutes under staff supervision. Within 6 months the improvement, not only in language and handwriting skills but in concentration and behaviour, was remarkable. I was convinced, that had the 'problem' been diagnosed at a much earlier stage most of these children would not have been labelled as behaviourally difficult, and they would not have been placed in an

1

The nerve cells have been numbered for illustrative purposes. If we assume that *1* is the site of instruction and the message is required to transfer to cell *7* the most direct route of transmission at 6 weeks is along the pathway connecting cells *1-2-4-5-6-8* and *7*. At 6 months the route is *1-6-7*. There are 7 operations in the younger child compared with 3 in the older child, therefore not only is the speed of information processing greatly increased but it is much less likely that information will be misdirected. At 6 months the developing infant will be able almost 'reflexively' to reach and secure a dangling ring, hold small cubes in either hand and assist with holding a feeder cup.

Usually, between the ages of 8 and 12 months, the infant has learned to co-ordinate not only his hands but also his feet. The child is able to crawl and can operate hands and feet in opposition. High kneeling follows and soon the child is able to achieve a standing position and walk independently.

There is evidence to suggest that in the case of the dyspraxic child the reinforced interconnections between nerve cells in the cerebral cortex are reduced in number. The cortex persists in a state of immaturity which varies greatly between individuals.

It seems reasonable, therefore, to suggest this as a possible explanation for the difficulties encountered by dyspraxic youngsters. They continue to require additional time to process information and concentration is often limited. The child is aware of his intention, but with the route between action and reaction so circuitous there is increased probability of the idea being lost along the way.

If we consider the function of the brain beyond the cerebral cortex it is possible that there may be other factors which explain some associated behaviours of dyspraxic children.

The cortex controls the body's sensory systems, its motor responses and the complex behaviours of thought and language. The cortex surrounds the limbic system which is responsible for actions relating to basic needs and emotions. The limbic system is the 'instinctive' part of the brain which is controlled by the cortex. If in dyspraxic children the cortex has fewer reinforced interconnections between the nerve cells, the control over the limbic system will also be reduced. Figure 2:4.

Fig. 2:4 *The limbic system in relation to the cerebral cortex*

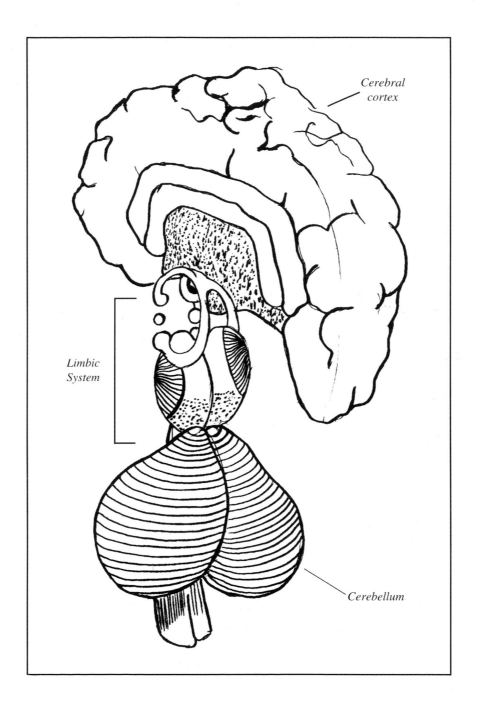

This is a possible explanation of the difficulty many dyspraxic children have in controlling their emotions, particularly during their early development and into primary education. They can become easily distressed, difficult to control and over-active.

To understand in greater detail the learning difficulties associated with dyspraxia it is necessary to consider how information is processed in the cortex.

The brain comprises a right and left hemisphere and they function in different ways. The left hemisphere processes information sequentially and is described as analytical because it specialises in recognising parts that make up a whole. Although it is most efficient at processing verbal information, language should not be considered to be 'in' the left hemisphere. This hemisphere is able to recognise that one stimulus comes before another and verbal perception and generation depend on the awareness of the sequence in which sounds occur.

While the left hemisphere separates out the parts that constitute a whole, the right specialises in combining the parts to create a whole. Unlike the left hemisphere which processes information in a linear manner, the right hemisphere organises simultaneously. It specialises in a method of processing that perceives and constructs patterns. It is more efficient at visual and spatial processing (images). Its language capacity is limited and words play little part in its functioning. Figure 2:5. While both hemispheres process sensory stimuli it is thought that non-verbal stimuli are processed primarily in the right hemisphere.

Fig. 2:5 *A visual representation of the functions of the two hemispheres*

Left hemisphere　　　　　　　　　**Right hemisphere**

Research into the specialisation of the right and left hemispheres shows that the effective processing of information requires access to both as they work to complement each other. Problems occur when a child is unable to utilise fully either or both hemispheres. By the time pupils reach secondary education they are expected to absorb most information from books and verbal discussions with their teachers. They work, in many instances, almost exclusively with words and numbers. Youngsters who are less able to process verbal information are required to learn in a way which is excessively difficult for them. Figure 2:6.

Fig. 2:6 *A diagrammatic representation of the processing differences between the left and right hemisphere.*

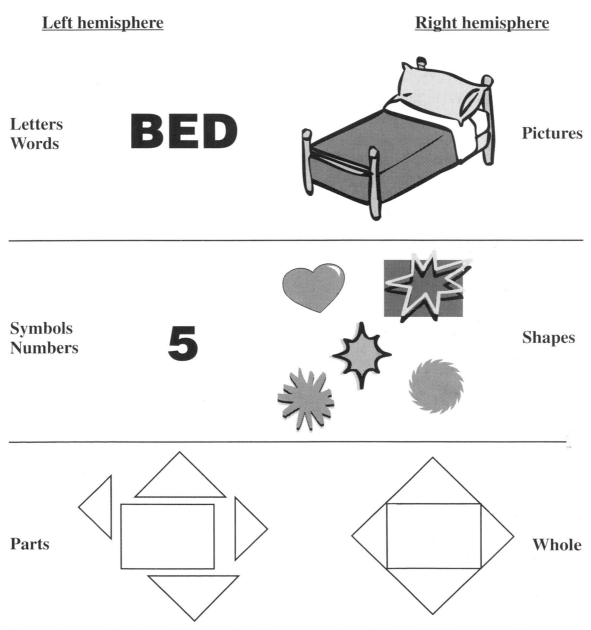

By understanding how information is conveyed and how it is interpreted, we can begin to examine assessment techniques which identify difficulties evident in this process experienced by dyspraxic youngsters.

Developmental
— Dyspraxia

As the child continues to progress towards recognised developmental milestones, some features emerge which are characteristic of youngsters subsequently diagnosed as dyspraxic. However, it is important to recognise that statements which are true in the majority of cases may not apply to every individual. It is crucial that all aspects of the child's development and achievements are considered before any diagnosis is given. The following tables detail the behaviours exhibited by a child of 6-12 months, 24 months and 36 months. Behaviours associated with dyspraxia are listed alongside. Descriptions of the child will always refer to he rather than he/she. The words <u>he</u> or <u>she</u> are interchangeable but the incidence of the condition is so predominantly male-biased the <u>he</u> convention seems most appropriate.

Fig. 3:2 Observable behaviours at 6 - 12 months

Social skills

Expected behaviours	Indications
Easily comforted by voice or adult physical contact	Takes time to be comforted. Can present as very irritable
Feeds well, contented after a meal	Feeding difficulties, colic reported after 3 months and milk allergies
Enjoys a variety of foods	Diet can be quite restricted
Adapts to good sleeping routine by 6 months	Sleeping difficulties. Seeks constant adult reassurance
Drinks from a feeder cup and finger-feeds	Food and other objects frequently mouthed
Enjoys having a bath	Can become distressed and show early dislike of water (up to 6 months)

Gross motor skills

Rolls from back to stomach Sits unaided Crawls on hands and knees Pulls up to standing position	Usually 'bottom shuffles' and either does not go through the crawling stage or passes through very briefly. Sometimes cannot sit unaided at 9 - 12 months
Makes purposeful arm and leg movements, e.g. moves to pick up toy and then spends time actively playing with it	High levels of motor activity. Repetitive arm and hand movements. Sometimes additional repetitive head movements - 'rolling and banging'

Fine motor skills

Able to pick up small toys with either hand. Uses thumb and first finger in opposition to do so. Passes toys between hands. Able to point with index finger	Picks objects using palmar 'fisted' grip. Finds it difficult to locate small objects and is unable to manipulate a toy in each hand

Language skills

Enjoys listening to music. Responds to adult requests like "Show me the ball". Some single words	Responds with distress to high noise level. No evidence of emerging language skills

Reasoning ability

Lifts toys from table and manipulates in direct line of vision. Shows interest by smiling or making babbling sounds. Shows awareness when toys are obscured from view, e.g. object hidden under a cup: child removes cup and shows understanding of the 'game'	May pick up a variety of toys but with fleeting interest. Moves from one to another after only a few seconds. Becomes irritated with 'hide and seek' game

Fig. 3:3 *Observable behaviour 12 - 24 months*

Social skills

Assists with dressing. He is able to remove shoes and socks and can take arms out of an unfastened coat	Shows no interest in dressing
Drinks from a handled cup appropriately and feeds with a spoon	Feeding continues to be messy. Limited control of spoon
Bladder control emerging, usually dry during the day	Often does not achieve toileting skills until 36+ months
Begins to share toys and work co-operatively with other children	Happy with his own company - isolated play. Exhibits extreme uncontrolled temper tantrums

Gross motor skills

Walks competently backwards and forwards and jumps from a low step, feet together	Often walking is not achieved until 18+ months. Child is not able to jump
Runs and is able to climb up and down stairs	Appears to be unsteady, falls easily and may move with a wide gait
Can kick a ball with either foot	Unable to lift one foot without overbalancing
Can throw a small ball with either hand	Difficulty directing movement

Fine motor skills

Starts to show preference for right or left hand	May not establish hand dominance until 4+ years
Plays constructively, building towers of 6+ bricks or stacking beakers. Replaces pegs into pegboard	Shows little interest in constructional activities. Finds tower building very difficult. Problems manipulating pegs and takes longer to complete the task
Enjoys water play, pouring between different containers	Enjoys water play but usually pours from container back into trough
Enjoys scribbling with crayons on paper. Can make horizontal, vertical and circular strokes	Has difficulty holding the crayon. Grip may be unnecessarily 'tight'

Language skills

Vocabulary comprising 20/30 words. Makes simple sentence construction like "There is the car"	May make initial sounds like 'mm' but has difficulty saying single words
Enjoys listening to stories and likes looking at books. Makes 'singing' noises and actions to some nursery rhymes	Interest in books may be fleeting. Listens to nursery rhymes but finds it difficult to make appropriate actions at the right time

Reasoning ability

Enjoys completing popular formboards with 3 insets. Can replace a ●, ■ and ▲	Has great difficulty manipulating shapes into the correct position. Becomes very frustrated and distressed
Constructs large 'Lego' pieces	Dislikes or avoids these activities

Fig. 3:4 *Observable behaviours 24 - 36 months*

Social skills

Uses a spoon and fork appropriately	Feeding continues to be messy. Prefers to use fingers
Beginning to form social relationships and play co-operatively with other children. Uses language to communicate, with additional use of gestures	Limited social communication; disadvantaged because of language difficulties. Continues to be emotional and easily distressed
Shared and singular activities extend to periods of 15 minutes	Unable to stay in one place for periods in excess of 2 - 3 minutes
Sleeps undisturbed for 10 - 12 hours	Sleeping difficulties may persist

Gross motor skills

Balance improves. child can stand on one foot for 6 - 10 seconds	Unable to balance on feet separately
Walks on tiptoes with arms moving loosely at either side	Walks on tiptoes with poor balance and hands showing associated mirror movements. (Arms move outwards and hands bend backwards from the inside
Able to ascend a climbing frame with confidence, placing one foot on each rung	Dislikes climbing activities. Can be anxious about heights
Performs running and jumping activities with arms held alongside body	Runs in unco-ordinated manner with arms above waist level. Exhibits high levels of motor activity
	May engage in repetitive behaviour such as hand clapping or vigorous rubbing of thumb against forefingers of both hands when excited

Fine motor skills

Able to copy simple shapes such a ●, ■ and †	May still be at the scribbling stage
Able to thread a sequence of large beads	Unable to co-ordinate this activity
Can cut out large shapes with scissors	Difficult to use as hand-dominance is not yet established. Look for associated movements with other hand

Language skills

Sentences extend to 6+ syllables "My dolly is called Meg"	Developing a single-word vocabulary. May frequently use the same sentence to generalise meaning, e.g. "Want drink" which may refer to any type of food. Uses gestures to convey meaning
Able to repeat some nursery rhymes and make appropriate actions	Unable to co-ordinate actions with rhyme. Loses interest easily
Enjoys looking at books and understands that the words convey meaning	Concentration presents major difficulties
Can follow commands such as "Put the car on the box"	Confuses 'on', 'in' and 'under'

Reasoning ability

Extended play with constructional toys. Enjoys 6+ piece formboards and simple jigsaws	Any activity which has a motor skill component is difficult and usually avoided
Beginning to have some concept of numbers. Can select the 'big' toy from choice of 2 or 3 items	Conceptual understanding is usually age-appropriate

Fig. 3:5 Summary of behaviours 0 - 3 years

- irritable and difficult to comfort - from birth

- feeding difficulties: milk allergies, colic, tolerates a restricted diet

- sleeping difficulties: problems establishing routine, requires constant adult reassurance

- delayed early motor development: sitting unaided, rolling from side to side, do not usually go through crawling stage as babies

- high levels of motor activity: constantly moving arms and legs

- repetitive behaviours: head banging or rolling

- sensitive to high levels of noise

- continued problems with development of feeding skills

- toilet training may be delayed

- avoids constructional toys such as jigsaws and Lego

- delayed language development: single words not evident until age 3

- highly emotional: easily distressed, frequent outbursts of uncontrolled behaviour

- concentration limited to 2/3 minutes on any task.

By the time the child reaches 3 parents may be aware that difficulties are emerging. Usually they have had concerns for some time but because developmental milestones were achieved, albeit at a slower rate than expected, they had been made to feel they were worrying without good cause and being 'over-anxious'. Parents usually have greater insight into their children's behaviour than 'professionals' and too frequently their concerns are minimised. Assessment of the youngster in a more structured setting, like nursery or play-group, may confirm parents' anxieties.

Between the age of 3 and 5 the child extends his skills, from the foundation which has been laid down during infancy. If the development of interconnections between nerve cells in the cortex is reduced, then the processing of information in the brain will be affected. The dyspraxic child will find more complex tasks increasingly difficult, and evidence can be obtained by observing his approaches to specified activities.

Observable behaviours between 3 and 5 years

Social skills

Dyspraxic children continue to present high levels of motor activity with limited concentration. They are often excluded from co-operative games enjoyed by other youngsters because their behaviour is too erratic. They find it difficult to remember more than two or three instructions and consequently cannot always remember the rules. Excitable behaviour is perceived by other children as immature and intentionally spoiling the game. Sensitivity to touch is poorly developed and dyspraxic children may be viewed as deliberately rough. They have difficulty determining their position in space and easily bump into others. This can be very irritating to other children in the group. The need to change activity frequently often results in wanting access to materials which are being used. Turn-taking is a problem because these children require immediate gratification. The disputes which follow farther remove the dyspraxic child from gaining acceptance within the class group.

Gross motor skills

The child may bump frequently into static objects. He may trip easily and appear accident-prone. Associated movements will be evident when motor activities are performed. The child is unable to separate out messages and direct them to particular limbs. Consequently, when running, both arms will be raised and the movement will appear unco-ordinated. Jumping and hopping also produce associated hand movements. Difficulties with hand-functioning can be observed. If the child is required to throw or catch a large ball he will be unable to stand still while doing so. If only one hand is involved in the throw the other performs similar movements like a six-week baby attempting to reach and grasp using both arms even when the toy is located on one side of the body. Even when the child is seated to perform manipulative tasks, like building or measuring, leg movements such as feet-tapping or swinging are characteristic of the dyspraxic child.

During outdoor play sessions the child prefers not to sit on the pedal toys as he will find it impossible to co-ordinate the required leg movements. The climbing frame is another source of anxiety as the child has poor figure-ground awareness and cannot gauge the height of the equipment. It may appear that the child is totally unconcerned for his safety as he launches himself from the uppermost level of the apparatus, but this apparent absence of fear is because at this stage he does not perceive the potential danger.

Fine motor skills

The snack table can be a distressing experience for the dyspraxic child if a routine is not established. Eating and holding a cup for drinking can still present major problems. Frequently the child is singled out by other youngsters because the drink always ends up either down his jumper or dripping from the edge of the table onto the floor. Jigsaws, formboards and other constructional toys are avoided as they are a major source of frustration. Although the child knows exactly how the pieces fit together his hands are unable to manipulate them. Dyspraxic youngsters have difficulty achieving a good pencil grip so drawing and colouring skills are immature. Copied shapes such as a circle and square are recognisable but are usually not joined, e.g. ☐ ◯ Drawings of people are recognisable but immature. Figure 3:6.

Fig. 3:6 Drawing of mummy by Andrew aged 4½.

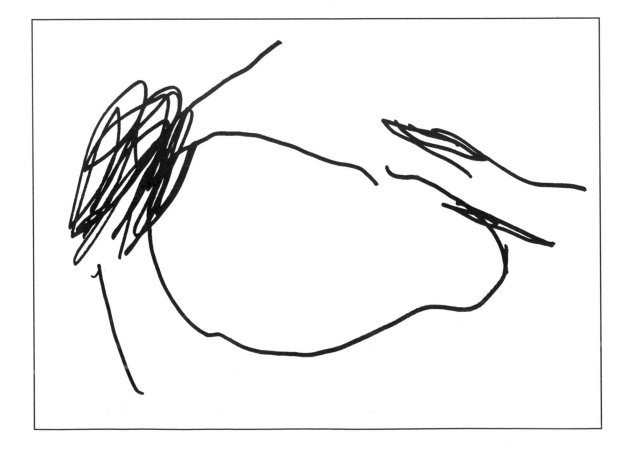

Laterality is not usually established until 5 - 6 years; when tracing around objects the dyspraxic child may draw round the right side of the shape with his right hand and then change to his left hand to complete the figure. He has difficulty crossing the mid-line and activities set out on the right side of the body will be performed with the right hand and conversely the left hand executes tasks positioned on the left.

Threading beads and using scissors to cut around large shapes are skills expected of a child transferring from nursery to reception class. Mastery of these tasks is not usually achieved by a dyspraxic child until 6-7 years.

Language skills

Verbal communication skills may be significantly delayed. Parents will express concern that speech cannot be understood by unfamiliar adults. The child may still be at the single-word level and even these words can be indistinct. The child will try to convey meaning using gestures and will become frustrated when they cannot be interpreted. Dyspraxic children have poor sound discrimination and will not be able to separate out verbal instructions if there is a high level of background noise. Voice tone may vary. Some children will appear to 'shout' most of the time and the pitch may alter if the child becomes excited. The dyspraxic child is emotional and exhibits frequent temper tantrums which reflect the mismatch between the child's understanding of the surrounding environment and his ability to operate control on it. Language development is slow and problems may continue to be evident until the child is well into primary education.

Reasoning ability

When a child experiences difficulty with perceptual and motor skills his reasoning ability is affected. It is important to recognise that the performance of these youngsters does not reflect their true intellectual ability.

The neural pathway along which information is transmitted in the dyspraxic child is a lengthy process, consequently the youngster executes instructions more slowly. If the children are asked to gather together for storytime, the dyspraxic child will continue to play in the water while the rest of the group responds to the request. This is not a deliberate act of defiance: it is merely a problem with the speed of information-processing. Poor concentration skills persist and many tasks are left unfinished. Dyspraxic children often lack creativity in play and this is yet another feature which isolates them from their peers and is further compounded by additional language difficulties.

Problems with sequencing and the conceptual understanding of 'time' are also characteristics of dyspraxic pre-school children. Events are described in the present tense and they may not understand the notion of 'morning' and 'afternoon'. If they are asked to sequence several shapes ranging from small to large a random pattern will often result. Sequencing picture cards to make a story will highlight similar problems. It is the organisation of the task and knowing where to begin which are the greatest obstacles. In addition the need to engage constantly in motor activity - swinging legs, clapping hands - distracts the child from successfully completing the task.

Fig. 3:7 *Summary of behaviours 3 - 5 years*

- very high levels of motor activity
  - feet swinging and tapping when seated
  - hands clapping or twisting
  - unable to stay in one place longer than 5 minutes

- very excitable
  - voice loud and shrill
  - easily distressed, temper tantrums

- move awkwardly
  - constantly bumping into objects and falling
  - associated mirror movements, hands flap when running or jumping

- difficulty pedalling tricycle or similar toy

- poor figure ground awareness
  - no sense of danger, jump from inappropriate heights

- continue to be messy eaters
  - often spill liquid from drinking cups
  - prefer to use fingers to feed

- avoid constructional toys
  - jigsaws
  - building blocks (Lego)

- poor fine motor skills
  - pencil grip
  - use of scissors
  - immature drawings

- lack of imaginative play
  - do not enjoy 'dressing up' or playing appropriately in the home corner or Wendy House

- limited creative play

- isolated in peer group
  - rejected by peers, prefer adult company

- laterality still not established
  - problems crossing mid-line

- language difficulties persist
  - children often referred to speech therapist

- sensitive to sensory stimulation
  - high levels of noise
  - dislike being touched or wearing new clothes

- limited response to verbal instructions
  - slower response time
  - problems with comprehension

- limited concentration
  - tasks often left unfinished.

The dyspraxic child is deemed to be failing long before he reaches the age of 5. Motor development and language skills are implicit in any assessment process at this age. Any test of cognitive ability relies heavily on the child's ability to respond verbally or execute the task manually. To score in a standardised assessment under the heading reasoning skills/cognitive ability, the child is required to:

0-12 months	**Hold cubes**
	Pass toys from hand to hand
	Throw objects
	Hold a pencil

12-24 months	**Show hand preference**
	Complete 3 piece formboards
	Scribble - draw horizontal lines
	Stack 4+ blocks

24-36 months	**Use scissors**
	Draw circles
	Insert pieces into 6-shape sorter
	Name a colour
	Repeat 3 digits

4 years	**Thread beads**
	Draw a simple figures of a person
	Count to 5
	Name 6 colours

5 years	**Draw recognisable pictures, e.g. house**
	Talk about the concept of time: yesterday, tomorrow
	Count 15+ bricks
	Manipulate blocks to complete a pattern (time-limit)

Consequently he will appear to have delayed cognitive skills if his ability is assessed using tests which have a bias towards language and motor skills to determine cognitive functioning.

Observable behaviours between 5 and 7 years

Problems which may have been identified previously by parents or teachers become more apparent and other difficulties may emerge. On entry to full-time education the child becomes part of a much more structured environment. Activities which might have been avoided in the nursery are an integral part of the daily routine.

Social skills

The routine itself may present significant problems for dyspraxic children. They find it difficult to sequence events and do not always remember to dress themselves in outdoor wear before going into the playground. They cannot understand why all the other children move back into school when the whistle is blown. The rest of the class is seated and ready to begin work with pencils out and pages opened before Danny returns from the cloakroom after spending 10 minutes struggling with his coat. He is upset anyway because he wasn't allowed to join a game of tag. He has been publically rebuked: "You can't run, you just push and spoil the game". Danny is questioned about his lateness: he can't find any reasons, his eye-contact is poor and he stares at the ceiling wondering perhaps what is on the menu for lunch. He is accused of not listening, and instructed to go to his seat.

Gross motor skills

While trying to listen intently to the next set of instructions he swings too far backwards on his chair. The class is disrupted again and Danny's 'behaviour' is becoming increasingly concerning for the class teacher. Unfortunately everyone has been directed to the hall for PE. Danny hates PE. Everyone laughs at him. Then unintentionally sexist directions are given which emphasise still further his failure to conform. "When the music starts I want the girls to walk round the outside of the hall and the boys to jump on the spot. When the music stops all change, boys walk round and girls jump".

The music starts and Danny enthusiastically begins to move with a quick marching step in a clockwise manner. He slowly realises that he is the only boy doing so. He slows down, trying to merge with the group in the centre and starts to jump. He hasn't realised that by this time the music has stopped and only the girls are jumping. The children are then divided into pairs. It has to be done that way because no-one would ever choose Danny as a partner. It is to be a simple catching game. A large soft ball is thrown from one child to the other. Danny can't properly judge the ball's position in space and the speed at which it travels. He stands with his legs in a wide, awkward stance and almost falls before the ball is thrown to him. His tongue is protruding and he licks his lips anxiously as he waits. The ball arrives and he flings his arms wildly into space. His arms cross somewhere in the region of his chest and his attempt to catch has sent the ball to the opposite end of the hall.

Fine motor skills

Danny was pleased to change out of his PE strip. He put on his trainers, with Velcro fasteners (he thought he would never be able to master the skills required to tie shoe laces) and thought it would be easier to tie the sleeves of his jumper around his waist than attempt to put it on. Back in the classroom he picked up his pencil to complete the maths, which was still unfinished. Danny knew how many fish to add to the line to make 14 but they looked more like tennis balls than sea creatures. His hand ached because he gripped his pencil so tightly. Sometimes there was even a slight tremor when he had to write or draw for a long time. His work always looked messy. The pencil seemed to make smudge marks all over the page. Even when the teacher wrote 'good work' or placed a 'sticker' at the end of the page he knew she didn't really mean it because it always looked so untidy. Sometimes Danny became so angry with his written work that he ripped it up and scribbled over it before anyone could see it. His name was barely legible, a mixture of upper and lower case letters. He just couldn't master the shapes.

Thank goodness it was lunch time. He supposed he would probably be at the back of the queue. Danny found it impossible to stand still and was always being accused of deliberately pushing into other children. Once he had fallen against the fire bell and the whole school was evacuated. When Danny started in the reception class he had enjoyed sitting down with the other children to eat. By the end of the first term no-one wanted to sit next to him. He was unable to co-ordinate a knife and fork and his food was usually scattered over the rest of the table. The problem was avoided when he changed from school dinners to packed lunch: sandwiches, crisps, an apple and a boxed drink with a straw presented fewer problems.

Language skills

Danny's verbal communication skills had improved considerably after having regular access to speech therapy. He was referred when he was 3 because his vocabulary comprised 10 indistinct words. His articulation was now age-appropriate but he would easily lose the thread of a conversation if more than 2 or 3 ideas were contained in a sentence. He still confused words when speaking

Developmental
── Dyspraxia

Observational assessment of the child's behaviour will give a general profile of ability. Social, motor, language and reasoning skills can be recorded at home and in the classroom. In addition, when a child is aged between 5 and 7 it is important to obtain more detailed information about cognitive ability and motor development as appropriate standardised assessments become available.

As outlined in chapter 2, motor movements reinforce the connections along selected neural pathways. Therefore it is the child's ability to execute specific motor tasks which gives an indication of the functioning in the cortex. As scans become more sophisticated they will enable clinicians to have specific information about particular areas of the brain. However, at present, the usual clinical approach to the study of brain functions remains the neurological examination. Information is obtained by examining motor patterns and the responses to testing of specific muscle groups. There are many standardised assessments available but the *Movement Assessment Battery for Children* - Henderson & Sugden is most commonly used. Children scoring below the 10th centile should be considered to exhibit a significant level of difficulty.

In addition, a full cognitive assessment should be completed. The Wechsler Intelligence Scales are standardised to be used with all school age children and adults and give the required information. However, many articles state that the single most important factor in the diagnosis of dyspraxia is the comparison of the scores between performance and verbal IQ, the latter being significantly higher. Sydney Chu in his article *The diagnosis of dyspraxia 1991*, expresses reservations with this 'diagnosis' as the test was not designed for this purpose. My research, which is detailed later, confirms the limitations of the discrepancy model of IQ scores. It is unhelpful to give the accumulative scores for verbal and performance IQ because that disguises the particular strengths in the child's cognitive profile. In addition the scaled scores in some of the sub-tests vary depending on the age of the child at the time of the assessment.

What is important, is to assess whether there are significant discrepancies between individual sub-test scores. Those which are consistently lower in dyspraxic youngsters are arithmetic, coding and block design. Even then, there are some dyspraxic pupils who do not fit this pattern of development and the final diagnosis depends on the experience of the clinician.

Fig. 3:9 *Summary of behaviours 5 - 7 years*

- problems adapting to a more structured school routine

- difficulties evident in PE

- slow at dressing - unable to tie shoe laces

- handwriting barely legible

- immature drawing - including copying skills

- limited concentration and poor listening skills

- literal use of language

- remember only 2/3 instructions

- classwork completed slowly

- continuing high levels of motor activity

- motor stereotypes - hand flapping or clapping when excited

- easily distressed, very emotional

- problems co-ordinating a knife and fork

- unable to form relationships with other youngsters and appear isolated in the class group

- sleeping difficulties - wake during the night and report nightmares

- may report physical symptoms - migraine, headaches, feeling sick.

Chapter
4

Assessing the junior age child

$\mathscr{P}$redominantly the youngsters referred for assessment are between the ages 7 and 11 and as recently as 1994 statistics indicate that most of them were in years 5 and 6. The major factor influencing the trend towards younger pupils is raised awareness of dyspraxia particularly on the part of parents.

There are many symptoms of the condition which are evident during the early years of development and by the time the child is 7 the full picture has usually emerged. This enables the assessor to make a more reliable diagnosis but parents and teachers often feel that because of their closeness to the child they should have been more aware of the difficulties and sought help earlier. Fortunately remediation programmes can be very effective, irrespective of the age of the child at the time of commencement.

The assessment is crucial because only when the areas of difficulty are identified can the appropriate remediation activities be selected.

Usually, the child will have been referred because:

● he appears to be a bright, able pupil who is verbally articulate but is unable to express himself adequately on paper
● he is exhibiting such extreme behavioural difficulties that his own work and that of the rest of the class is suffering.

Early development

The starting point of any assessment is obtaining an accurate profile of the child's early developmental history. Determine whether there were any significant factors at an earlier age which may have contributed to the present difficulties. Have there been any medical problems?

What are the views of parents and teachers and what are the major areas of concern?

Attainment tests

The typical pattern emerging would be a youngster who displays a range of strengths and weaknesses. In 60% of the cases referred to me during the past 6 years, the pupils achieved reading ages (as measured using standardised tests) at or above their chronological age. However, when the child was asked to read aloud in many cases the delivery was hesitant, without punctuation, and showed a misuse of tone and pitch.

Spelling presented greater levels of difficulty, with only 15% of pupils in the sample achieving a level commensurate with or above their chronological age.

Assessment of handwriting

Assessment of handwriting skills is one of the factors which contributes to the diagnosis of dyspraxia. Speed of handwriting, pencil grip and muscle tone in the fingers should be recorded and, in addition, information about letter formation. In 90% of the diagnosed cases of dyspraxia in the sample particular features were evident. The child preferred to print rather than join up letters. The words were a mixture of upper and lower case letters with little or no punctuation. The pupil's lack of perception of space and shape was evident when words were started on one line, perhaps with only the first letter, and finished on the next. There was little evidence of spacing between words. Figure 4:1 is an example to illustrate these features.

Fig. 4:1 *Sam, aged 11*

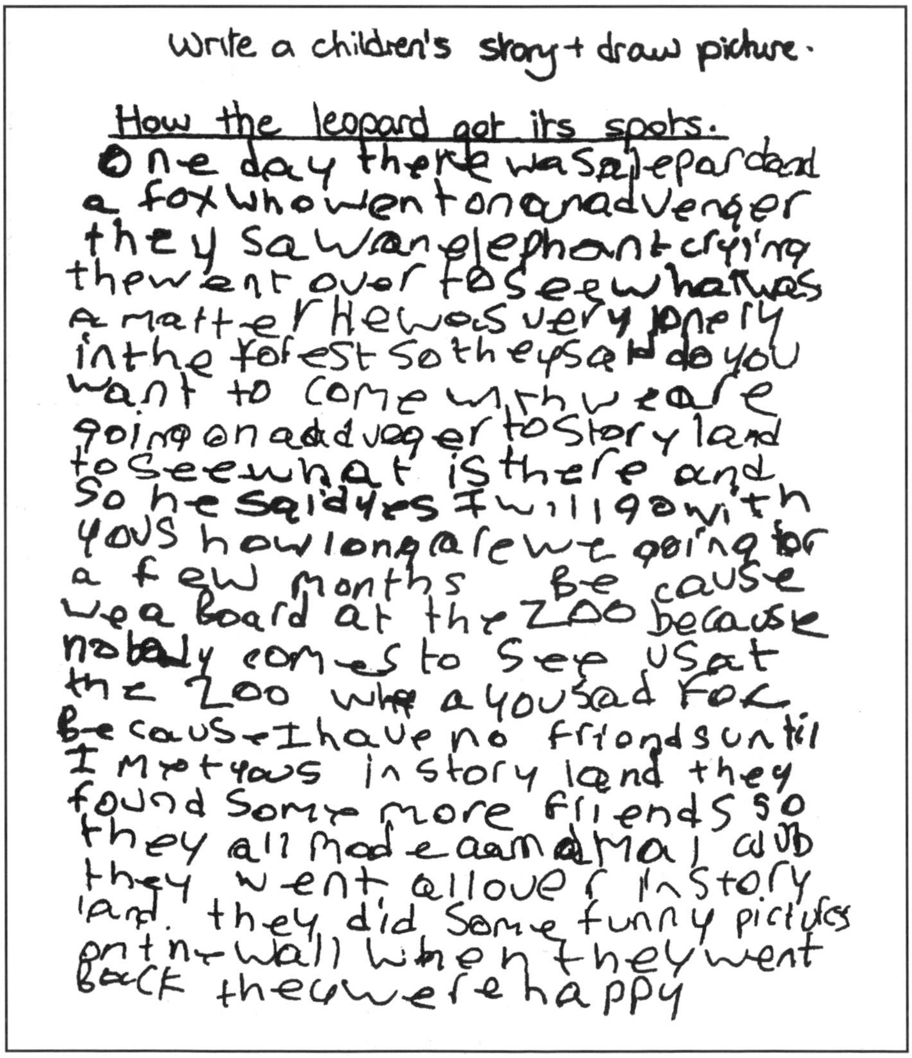
Write a children's story + draw picture.

How the leopard got its spots.
One day there was a leopard and
a fox who went on a advenger
they saw an elephant crying
the went over to see what was
a matter He was very lonely
in the forest so they said do you
want to come with we are
going on a advenger to story land
to see what is there and
so he said yes I will go with
yous how long are we going for
a few months be cause
we a board at the zoo because
nobody comes to see us at
the zoo whe a you sad fox
because I have no friends until
I met yous in story land they
found some more friends so
they all made a animal club
they went allover in story
land. they did some funny pictures
on the wall when they went
back they were happy

Although the child's conceptual understanding of mathematics may be within the average expected for his age, the ability to translate this understanding and record it manually is impaired. If the child sets out the numbers incorrectly on the page it is unlikely that he will arrive at the correct answer. See Figure 4:2.

Fig. 4:2 Matthew, aged 8

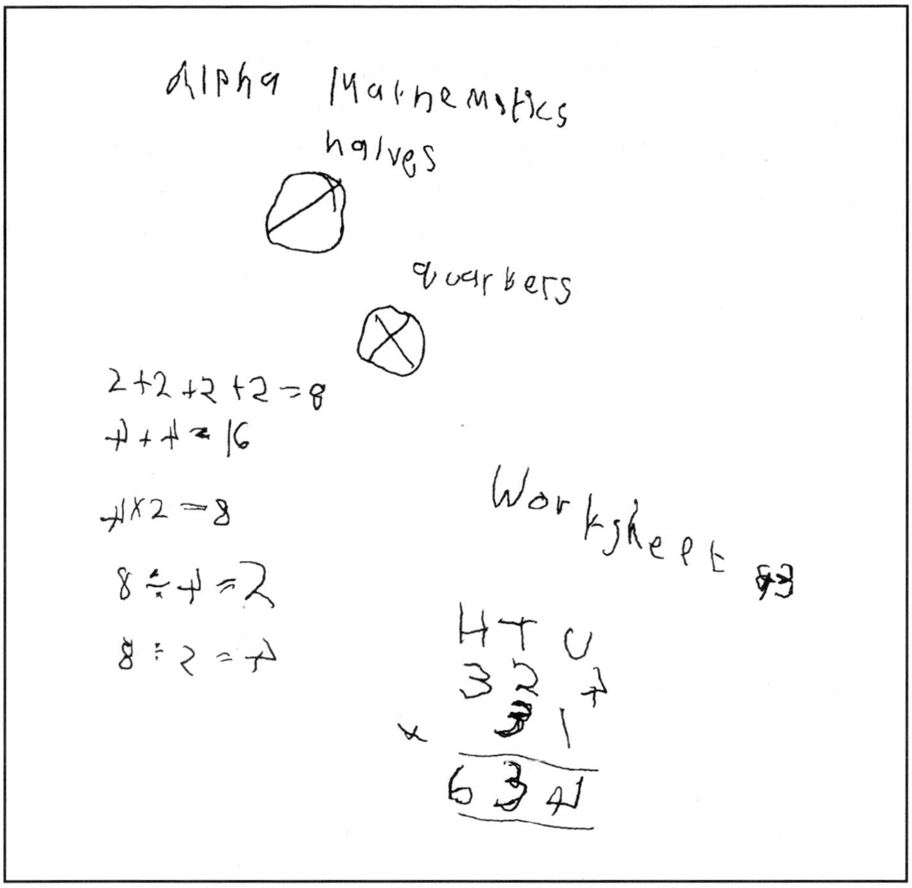

Matthew, sets out some multiplication and division sums on the left side of the page. The second calculation 4 x 4 shows an incorrectly angled multiplication sign which reads 4 + 4. When the exercise is marked Matthew will not understand why this is incorrect. He knows 4 x 4 = 16. Why has the teacher marked it with a cross? In the next worksheet again Matthew cannot find a mistake. He placed 4 in the units column, then added 1 + 2 resulting in 3 being placed in the tens column and 3 + 3 makes 6. Matthew had taken much longer to complete the work than other members of his class. It had taken an hour and a great amount of effort to produce it. He was beginning to wonder whether it was worth the bother, most of it was wrong anyway.

Cognitive assessment

The Weschler Intelligence Scale for Children (WISC) gives a comprehensive profile of the child's verbal and non-verbal ability. It enables the clinician to assess the intellectual ability of children aged from 6 years to 16 years 11 months. David Weschler himself sounded a note of caution when he stated in 1979 that "Intellectual ability is only one aspect of intelligence. Those who are responsible for interpreting the results of intelligence testing must be careful to distinguish between test scores or IQs on one hand and intelligence on the other". The purpose of the Weschler assessment is to obtain a broad sample from an individual's full array of cognitive abilities, to determine areas of particular strength or weakness. This assessment of neuro-psychological function, i.e. the pattern of behaviours which give information as to how the brain is operating, is confirmed by Kaplan, Fein, Morris and Delis in their 1991 report that the qualitative interpretation of the individual performance in the sub-tests supports the notion that the Weschler Intelligence Scales can be neuropsychological instruments.

The WISC III comprises 13 sub-tests which are divided into assessments of verbal and non-verbal ability. Figure 4:3.

Fig. 4:3

Verbal scores	Performance scores (Non-verbal)
Information	Picture completion
Similarities	Coding
Arithmetic	Picture arrangement
Vocabulary	Block design
Comprehension	Object assembly
(Digit span)	(Symbol search)
	(Mazes)

The sub-tests identified in brackets are supplementary but provide important additional information if they are completed.

Format and purpose of each sub-test

Information

The child is asked to respond verbally to a series of questions which assess his general knowledge. They reflect how well information about the environment is absorbed. As the child progresses through primary and on into secondary education he is expected to absorb more factual data from books. The pupil with reading difficulties may have problems with this test.

Similarities

The child is presented with two words such as 'chair' and 'table' and asked to say why they are the same. This reflects the child's understanding of language. The child is encouraged to give as much detail as possible in his response.

Arithmetic

This test relates to the child's general intellectual ability and he is required to respond orally to questions of mental arithmetic. Some youngsters perform much better when giving verbal responses than when required to write down the answer.

Vocabulary

The child is asked to give the definitions of a series of single words and is encouraged to give as much information as possible. He often inserts the word into a sentence to convey the meaning.

Comprehension

The child is presented with a series of questions beginning "What should you do if ...". The responses give an indication of the child's social code. This assessment differs from reading comprehension tests where the child is asked questions which relate to the passage in which the answer can be found.

Digit span

The child is asked to repeat a series of numbers of increasing length forwards and backwards. They measure his short-term ability to retain auditory sequential information. This test requires concentration and can present difficulties for children with attention deficits.

Picture completion

A series of coloured pictures is presented to the child and he is asked to identify which part is missing. This sub-test assesses the child's ability to concentrate and analyse data visually presented to him.

Coding

Younger children are required to draw a symbol inside a series of simple shapes. Older children (8+) copy symbols under a series of numbers. Youngsters with a poor short-term visual memory or significant visual motor problems experience particular difficulty with this sub-test because they are required to concentrate and co-ordinate eye and hand movements at speed.

Picture arrangement

A set of cards with a picture on each is mixed up and presented to the child. He is required to rearrange them into the sequence which correctly relates the story. This assesses the child's visual sequencing ability.

Block design

Initially the child is given 4 cubes and,then as the designs become more complicated, 9 cubes. A two-dimensional pattern is placed in front of the child who is then required to reproduce it using the cubes. This assesses the child's visual perceptual skills.

Object assembly

A set of jigsaw pieces is presented to the child who is required to assemble them in a recognisable form. The tasks become increasingly complex. This measures the child's ability to organise visually presented material into a whole from its component parts.

Symbol search

A series of paired groups of symbols is positioned on the left side of the page. The child scans the row to determine whether the symbols are present farther along. This requires concentration and the ability to co-ordinate eye movement to scan the page at speed.

Mazes

The child is given a starting point and using a pencil works his way through without crossing any of the lines. Good hand-eye co-ordination is needed.

The profile of scores achieved in the sub-tests of the WISC III can vary from one child to another. Some youngsters achieve such very low scores in some areas that it is unhelpful to calculate their overall verbal and performance intelligence quotient. What must be considered is whether there is a wide discrepancy between sub-test scores. Scaled scores achieved by dyspraxic youngsters vary according to age (see chapter 5) but some tests appear to present particular difficulties in more than 90% of dyspraxic youngsters: they are arithmetic, coding and block design. Figures 4:4 and 4:5 represent two profiles.

Fig. 4:4 Jenny, aged 7.4

WISC III profile

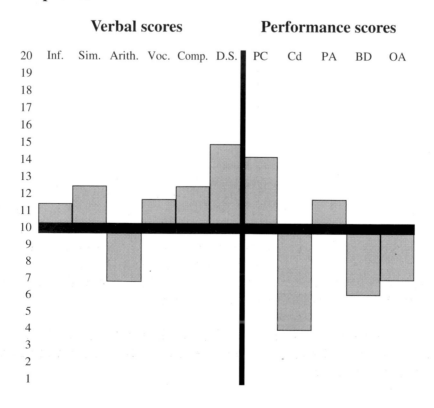

Interpretation

The scaled scores range from 1-19 where 10 is the average. Scores between 9 and 11 are in the average range. In the sub-tests administered, Jenny has achieved average scores in 3, above average in 4 and below average in 4. The assessment shows that in 7 out of 11 sub-tests, Jenny's ability is average to above average. If the scores are converted into an intelligence quotient Jenny has a verbal score of 107 and a performance score of 88 which suggests that her ability is average to low average. To ensure that Jenny has access to a curriculum which is stimulating, her strengths must be recognised and her specific visual perceptual and visual motor difficulties identified.

Fig. 4:5 Paul, aged 10.2

WISC III profile

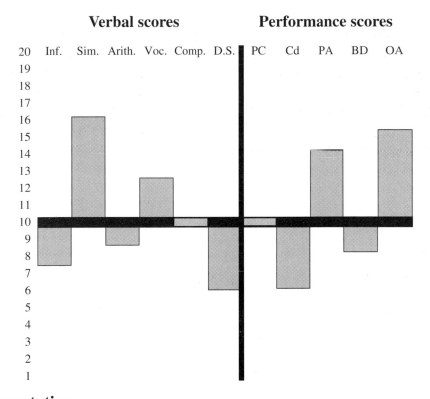

Interpretation

In the sub-tests administered Paul has achieved average scores in 3, above average in 4, and below average in 4. Like Jenny, Paul's ability is average to above average in 7 out of 11 sub-tests. Paul's verbal IQ is 101 and his performance IQ is 104. Contrary to some definitions of the criteria for a diagnosis of dyspraxia, Paul's performance score is higher than his verbal score. However, like Jenny, Paul has visual perceptual and visual motor problems but, in contrast, his visual sequencing is very good. The assessment also highlighted some difficulties with Paul's short-term auditory memory.

The cognitive assessments of Paul and Jenny showed that although they presented similar patterns of behaviour there were operational differences in the way they processed information.

Motor skills screening

The neuropsychological assessment of cognitive function does not in itself provide sufficient information to diagnose dyspraxia, as profiles vary markedly between individuals. Other factors which must be considered are:

● early developmental history

● curriculum attainments

● handwriting

● language development

● social/life skills.

The final part of the assessment is to evaluate the child's motor skills. As outlined in chapter 2, motor patterns and the responses of specific muscle groups to testing give additional information about the way the brain is functioning. The child's performance in each of the sub-tests must be accurately recorded.

The purpose of the motor skills screening is to identify major deficits and observe whether they follow a pattern. For example, the child may exhibit predominantly left-sided difficulties. This would suggest that the region of concern is the right hemisphere. (The right hemisphere controls the left side of the body and vice-versa). This may confirm details from previous assessments if the child appears to have poor perceptual skills (right hemisphere activity) in comparison with age - appropriate language development.

The tests most frequently used to assess motor skills are:

● The Bruininks - Oseretsky Test of Motor Proficiency

● Movement Assessment Battery for Children.

These assessments are comprehensive but can take in excess of an hour to administer. After working extensively with both, I compiled the Motor Skills Screening which selects some activities from each and contains additional items from the Fog Test which screens for neurological difficulties. The Motor Skills Screening enables the assessor in approximately 20 minutes to identify youngsters aged 7+ who exhibit motor difficulties. The results from this screening, in addition to the cognitive assessment and the developmental history of the child, would confirm the diagnosis of dyspraxia.

Fig. 4:6

Motor Skills Screening

Name...Date..........................Age.................

Activity	Behaviour	Date
1. Walking on toes forwards and backwards		
2. Walking on heels forwards and backwards		
3. Walking on insides of feet		
4. Walking on outsides of feet		
5. Recognising fingers touched when obscured from view. Right hand then left		
6. Finger sequencing - right then left		
7. Wrist rotation		
8. Balancing on each foot		
9. Touching end of nose with index finger of each hand (eyes closed)		
10. Jumping, feet together		

This proforma enables the assessor to record the behaviours observed during the assessment. It is important that all indications are detailed so that an effective remediation programme can be produced. Look for all associated mirror movements and other physical signs such as tremors or tongue -thrusting.

Instructions for the administration of the screening and sketches of the behaviour associated with motor difficulties are given in Figure 4:7.

Fig. 4:7

Using the Motor Skills Screening the following behaviours would indicate a motor difficulty.

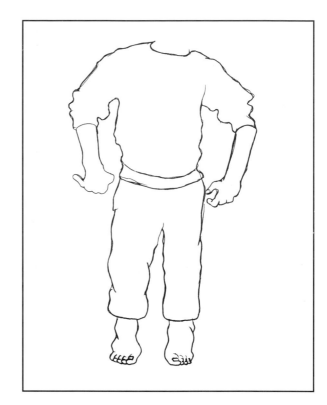

Activity

1. Walking on toes

Behaviour

Arms move outwards and hands bend at the wrist away from the body

Activity

2. Walking on heels

Behaviour

Arms held upwards from the elbow, hands bend upwards towards the body

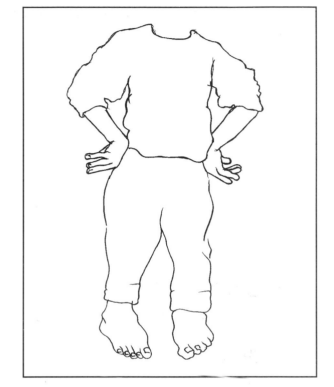

Activity

3. Walking on insides of feet

Behaviour

Arms extended behind, hands bend turning away from the body

Activity

4. Walking on outsides of feet

Behaviour

Arms bend outwards and wrists turn in

Activity

5. Obscure the fingers of one hand and the examiner touches two simultaneously. Ask the child to point out (with the other hand) those touched
Record 5 times with each hand

Behaviour

The child is consistently unable to identify the correct fingers

Activity

6. Ask the child to sequence each finger against the thumb of the same hand, slowly at first then more quickly. Test each hand separately then try hands together

Behaviour

Look for associated movements with the relaxed hand. Usually the child mirrors the activity

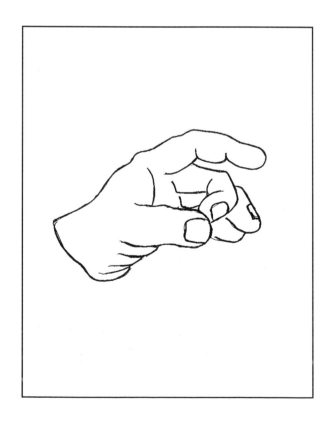

Activity

7. Demonstrate and ask the child to rotate both wrists simultaneously with the thumbs moving towards and then away from each other

Behaviour

See whether the child can rotate his wrists without his elbows moving outwards

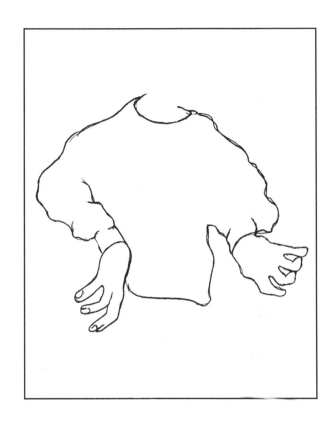

Activity

8. Ask the child to balance on each foot

Behaviour

The child should be able to achieve 10+ seconds on each foot

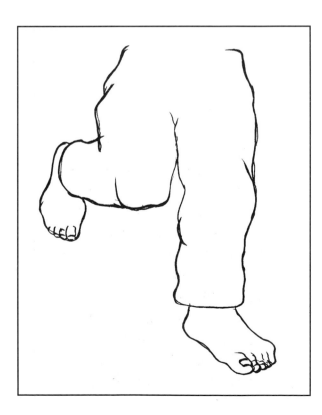

Activity

9. Demonstrate by standing in front of the child and make a wide arc first with the right hand and then the left and touch the end of your nose with the index finger of each. Make sure that eyes are closed

Behaviour

Child will probably distract the examiner by coughing at the last minute or will touch his nose with the whole of his hand

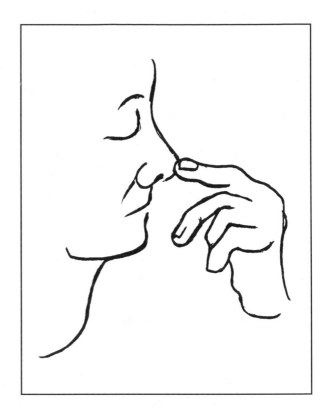

Activity

10. Ask the child to jump repeatedly with feet together

Behaviour

Problems will be observed in establishing the jumping routine. Elbows held tightly into waist, arms upwards and fists clenched

The assessments described in this chapter are also appropriate for youngsters in secondary education. Although the results in the cognitive profile follow a similar pattern, motor difficulties may become less evident.

Between the ages of 7 and 11 dyspraxic children develop strategies for survival. They have been excluded from their peer group and they strive desperately to belong. Some accept their isolation but develop school phobia. They complain of frequent headaches and stomach pains which rarely occur during holiday periods. Alternatively, they may be easily led and are directed to misbehaviour by the group leaders in the class. They accept that any attention, even if it is negative, is better than total exclusion.

Concentration is a major problem for dyspraxic youngsters, particularly during their primary school years. With access to a greater variety of curricular subjects in secondary education it is probable that in some subjects their attention will be improved. However, in later school years the dyspraxic child exhibits more extensive behavioural difficulties and is much more likely to suffer from depression.

Dyspraxic children continue to be extremely emotional and motor stereotypes such as hand-flapping persist when they become anxious or excited. The symptoms continue even when the children move on to further education. They do not 'grow out of it' and can benefit from remediation programmes even if they are not diagnosed until well into their teens.

Developmental Dyspraxia

Chapter
5

Research

$\mathcal{T}$his chapter examines data collected between 1988 and 1995 and determines the relationships between the assessment information and the youngsters' cognitive abilities, educational attainments and behaviour.

The sections consider:

- profiles of pupils using the Wechsler Pre-school and Primary Scale of Intelligence Revised (WPPSI-R UK) the Wechsler Intelligence Scale for Children III (WISC-III) and the Wechsler Adult-Intelligence Scale (WAIS)

- a study of 8 pupils aged between 5 years 3 months and 6 years 8 months in an infants school

- a study of 7 secondary pupils aged between 11 years 3 months and 13 years 9 months in a comprehensive school

- the case study of a child selected from the sample of additional individual profiles of youngsters aged between 3 years 4 months and 18 years 5 months.

Pupil profiles using the Wechsler Intelligence Scales

The Wechsler Scales enable the assessor to measure cognitive abilities of children from the age of 3 to adulthood. There is continuing debate about the reliability of instruments which measure those abilities in children under school age (3-5) because assessment using a developmental checklist, for example, can reflect the child's access to external factors rather than assess his 'potential'. A child who has not had access to a bike will not be able to pedal, a child who has not been encouraged to examine shapes and complete inset puzzles initially will not excel at fitting jigsaw pieces together, knowledge of colours is dependent on the child having them named to him.

As the tasks in developmental assessments become more complex they align more closely with those found in standardised intelligence tests like the WPPSI. This comparison can be made if we consider the eye-hand co-ordination task of the Griffiths Mental Developmental Scales (Year III) and the Geometric Design section of the WPPSI. Both require the child to draw horizontal and vertical lines and reproduce a cross and a circle.

Developmental ———————————————————
—— **Dyspraxia**

Although abilities such as spatial awareness, perceptual skills and language development are emerging by the age of 3 and can be measured successfully using psychometric assessments, dyspraxic children are severely disadvantaged. As outlined in chapter 3 where developmental profiles were discussed at length, many emerging skills which could be expected to be present by the age of 3 do not develop until 5 or 6. This is confirmed by the results achieved by dyspraxic youngsters in psychometric tests. The WISC profiles alter with the age of the child. However, it is the magnitude of the deficit in significant sub-tests which alters, rather than the child's general ability profile.

The data on which these statements are made comprise a total of 243 WPPSI-R, WISC-RS, WISC III and WAIS record forms. From this sample 27 forms were incomplete and could not be included. A further 9 were excluded because the pupils had diagnosed medical conditions which included epilepsy and hydrocephalus.

The remaining 207 assessments were categorised:

- 23-WPPSI (16 male, 7 female) age range 3.4 years - 7.2 years

- 139 WISC-RS (126 male, 13 female) age range 7.7 years - 15.3 years

- 34 WISC III (28 male, 6 female) age range 6.4 years - 16.8 years

- 11 WAIS (5 male, 6 female) age Range 16.2 years - 18.5 years.

There were 175 males and 32 females in the sample, a ratio of 5:1.

Figure 5:1 shows average scaled scores achieved in each sub-test for the total sample population. Names of the sub-tests are derived from the WISC-III but the geometric design (WPPSI) and the digit symbol (WAIS) are scored with the coding sub-test.

Fig 5:1

*Average scaled scores achieved in the total sample population
(ages 5-16) in the sub-tests of the WPPSI, WISC-RS, WISC-III and WAIS*

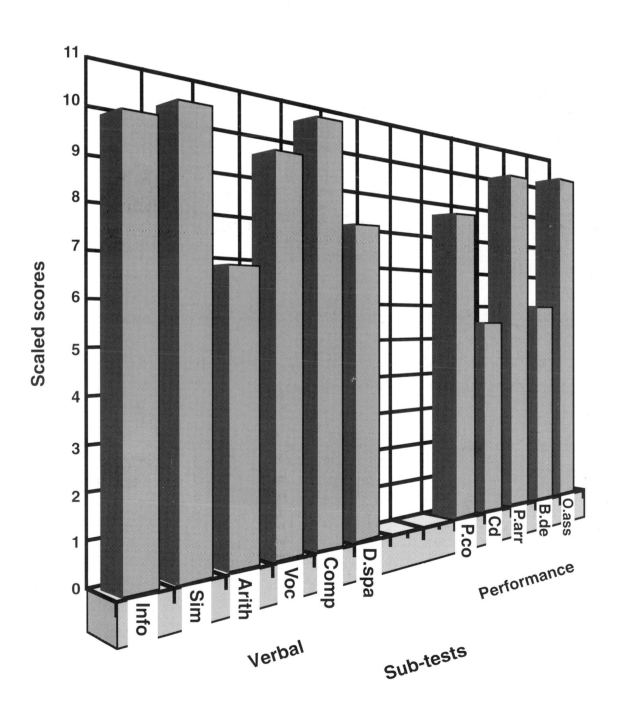

Average values for each sub-test were:

Verbal scores

Information	9.64
Similarities	10.2
Arithmetic	6.76
Vocabulary	9.53
Comprehension	10.5
Digit span	8.0

Performance scores

Picture completion	8.59
Coding	5.53
Picture arrangement	10.00
Block design	6.06
Object assembly	10.17

If the arithmetic and digit span sub-tests are excluded the average value of summed verbal scores = **10.12**

If the coding and block design sub-tests are excluded the average value of summed performance scores = **9.64**

The average value of arithmetic, digit span, coding and block design sub-test scores = **6.65**

The average score achieved in the digit span sub-test appears to increase with the age of the pupil and will be discussed later in this chapter. However, the population sample for this age is just 11 pupils so the statistical evidence is extremely limited.

What emerges from this analysis is that the neuropsychological assessment does identify specific weaknesses, certainly in 3 areas and possibly one other. Therefore, we should not consider the discrepancy model of the performance IQ being lower than the verbal IQ as a diagnosis of dyspraxia. What we can say is that if the scaled scores in the sub-tests of arithmetic, coding, block design and digit span are significantly depressed in relation to the scores in the other sub-tests, then these are indications that the child is dyspraxic.

If the magnitude of the weakness is greater in block design and coding than in the arithmetic and digit span sub-tests, obviously the performance IQ will be lower. However, there are many examples of the converse occurring, thus showing a depressed verbal IQ. It is the individual sub-test profile which is significant, not the overall IQ.

Fig 5:2

*Average scaled scores achieved in each of the WISC-RS and WISC-III
(age 6-16)*

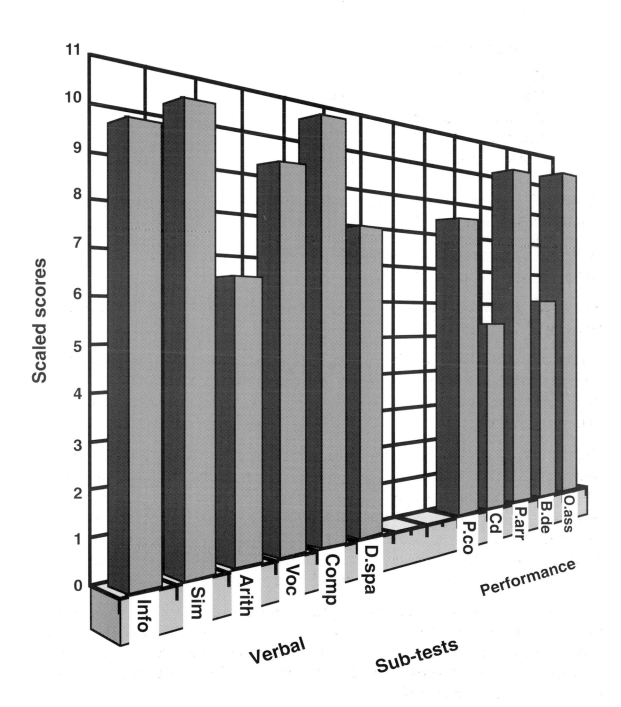

Figure 5:2 shows the average scaled scores achieved in each sub-test by pupils assessed using the WISC-RS and WISC III. The sample comprises 173 pupils from the total of 207. As expected, because the sample size is 83% of the total the results follow similar pattern to those in the whole population.

Average values for each sub-test were:

Verbal scores

Information	9.58
Similarities	10.27
Arithmetic	6.51
Vocabulary	9.2
Comprehension	10.5
Digit span	7.9

Performance scores

Picture completion	8.46
Coding	5.47
Picture arrangement	10.08
Block design	6.13
Object assembly	10.29

If the arithmetic sub-test is excluded the average value of summed scores = **9.43**

If the coding and block design sub-tests are excluded the average value of summed performance scores = **9.61**

The average value of arithmetic, coding and block design sub-test scores = **6.04**

Fig 5:3

Average scaled scores achieved in each sub-test of the WPPSI
(age 3-7 years)

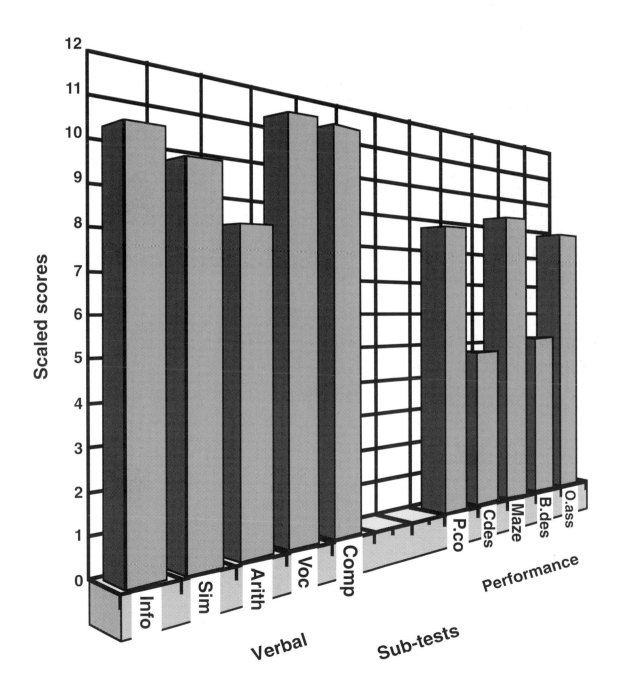

Developmental
—Dyspraxia

The analysis of sub-test scores of completed WPPSI assessments shows a similar pattern, but verbal scores on average are higher than performance. This information is based on a sample of 23 pupils, 16 boys and 7 girls.

Figure 5:3 shows the average scaled scores achieved in each sub-test. Although arithmetic, geometric design (coding equivalent) and block design are again the most significantly depressed scores, the verbal scores are on average higher and the performance scores lower than the full population sample. Average values for each sub-test were:

Verbal scores

Information	10.3
Similarities	9.7
Arithmetic	8.3
Vocabulary	11.2
Comprehension	11.1

Performance scores

Picture completion	8.7
Geometric design	4.8
Mazes	9.2
Block design	5.2
Object assembly	8.8

If the arithmetic sub-test is excluded the average value of summed verbal scores = **10.58**

If the geometric design and block design sub-tests are excluded the average value of summed performance scores = **8.9**

Average value of arithmetic, geometric design and block design sub-test scores = **6.1**

There can be many explanations as to why the performance scores are more depressed in the younger child. It is probable that the motor component is more significant at this level so that any test with an eye-hand co-ordination component which is assessing a perceptual skill presents major problems for the child.

The profile of achievement from the WAIS is based on the assessment of 11 pupils, 5 boys and 6 girls. The ratio of boys to girls suggests that this is not a representative population sample of youngsters at this age. I do not intend, therefore, to draw any particular conclusions from the sub-test scores but present them only for information. Of the 11 pupils, 7 were referred from colleagues in further education, 2 were self-referrals and 2 were parental referrals via the general practitioner.

Fig 5:4

Average scaled scores achieved in each sub-test of the WAIS
(age 16-18)

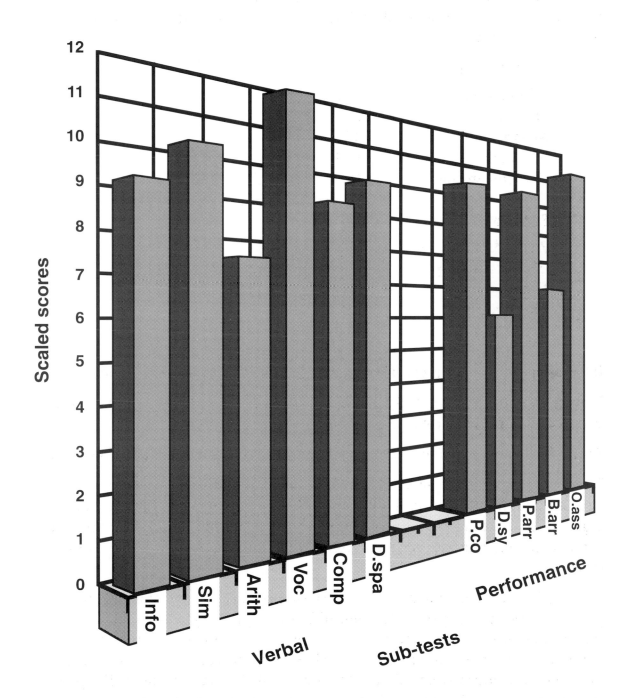

Figure 5:4 shows that the significant deficit areas continue to be arithmetic, digit symbol (coding) and block design. In this small sample the average score for the digit span sub-test does not appear to be particularly low in relation to the other verbal scores.

Verbal scores

Information	9.2
Similarities	10.1
Arithmetic	7.5
Vocabulary	11.7
Comprehension	9.1
Digit span	9.8

Reference scores

Picture completion	10.3
Digit symbol (coding)	6.1
Picture arrangement	10.2
Block design	7.0
Object assembly	11.1

If the arithmetic sub-test is excluded, the average value of summed verbal scores = **9.98**

If the digit symbol and block design sub-tests are excluded the average value of summed performance scores = **10.53**

The average value of arithmetic, digit symbol and block design sub-test scores = **6.8**

All the youngsters in this sample population were referred for assessment because concerns had been raised by parents or teachers about their school attainments and/or behaviour. The ratio of boys to girls differs in each age band. In the pre-school and infants group (3-7 years) the ratio is approximately 2:1. When the children move into the junior classes and on into secondary education the ratio is much more heavily skewed towards the boys, approximately 8:1. Then in further education the numbers are usually equal.

If we analyse specific reasons for referral in the early years (up to 7), parents express concerns that their children have been slow to achieve some developmental milestones and are becoming isolated within their peer group. Problems with concentration, language development and poor co-ordination are identified as major difficulties at this age and the ratio of 2:1 is probably an accurate reflection of the incidence in the population. After the age of 7 there is greater need for boys to develop good motor skills to achieve acceptance within the peer group. Despite equal opportunity policies, observation still indicates that boys are more likely to engage in team games such as football, while girls prefer to spend time in smaller groups. Soon there are more displays of behavioural difficulties which are merely the outlet of increasing frustration. Children who present behavioural problems in the classroom are quickly identified. The problems transfer to secondary education where truancy may become a major problem. Hence the ratio of 8:1 for this age group does not suggest that the dyspraxic proportion has changed but merely that boys are more likely to be identified.

So what can be the explanation for equal numbers of males and females referred after the age of 16? One may assume that a greater proportion of dyspraxic males become so disaffected with the 'system' that they do not consider further courses of study, so the ratio 1:1 in the sample may be an accurate reflection for the post-16 age group.

Controlled intervention study involving pupils aged between 5 years 3 months and 6 years 8 months

Background information

The headteacher and staff at a local infants school were becoming increasingly concerned about the number of pupils entering the reception class who had significant problems with concentration, organisation of work and appeared to exhibit fine and gross motor co-ordination difficulties. Some of the children had older brothers and sisters who had presented similar profiles at the same age, many of whom continued to experience subsequent learning difficulties.

In September 1993 one of the teaching members of staff, who was aware of the increasing incidence in the diagnosis of dyspraxia, embarked on a project to identify pupils who had deficits in attention with additional motor and perceptual difficulties, and provide them with daily access to activities designed to remediate their problems.

Pupil selection

The class teachers of the pupils aged between 5 and 7 were asked to identify children in their group who displayed any of the following:

- language difficulties
- immature drawing skills - unable to draw recognisable shapes or pictures
- poor pencil control

- appeared unco-ordinated when running
- limited concentration
- problems remembering instructions
- difficulty working with other pupils
- a mismatch between general understanding and the ability to record or convey information
- highly sensitive.

Parents of the children identified were contacted and given information about the purpose of the intervention. All agreed that if selected their child could participate in the programme.

Initially, 10 pupils, (4 girls and 6 boys) were identified. I completed a more detailed screening using the Wechsler Pre-school and Primary Scale of Intelligence and the Motor Assessment Battery for Children. One pupil was absent from school on the day of my visit and another had generalised rather than specific learning difficulties. Therefore the final sample comprised 2 girls and 6 boys, each showing varying degrees of dyspraxia.

At the outset 2 samples of handwritten work were collected from each pupil. One was a piece of 'free' writing and the other a section from the child's arithmetic book.

Intervention

Children selected worked together as a group and each had access to activities to extend their immature motor skills. The purpose of the exercises was to reinforce the development of neural pathways in the brain which in time would improve the child's cognitive ability and eye-hand co-ordination.

The teaching and auxilliary staff were involved with the programme which took 20 minutes every day to complete. After the baseline behaviour was established for each child, targets were set individually for every activity and progress was recorded daily and reassessed at the end of each week.

Intervention began in the last week of September 1993 and continued until the December holiday. The next term was a time for consolidation of newly-acquired skills. The exercises recommenced in April 1994 and continued until June 1994.

Activities

There was some variation of ability between the pupils in the group and this was reflected in the activities. The programme is detailed on page

A number of adults were involved in monitoring the pupils as they moved from one activity to another so the instructions had to be specific to ensure continuity from one day to the next.

1. **Skipping rope**

   A skipping rope 3 metres in length is secured at one end, (tied to a handle or wall bar). The child is positioned far enough away so that when he is holding the free end the centre of the rope just touches the floor.

   Making a large arc, the rope is turned clockwise 30 times with the right hand and then anti-clockwise with the left.

   Record how many times the movement breaks down before 30 turns are achieved.

2. **Measured line**

   It is important that the distance remains constant so that improvements in behaviour can be recorded accurately.

   Mark a line 2cm wide and 7 metres long.
   - a) The child walks along heel to toe, each foot in turn
   - b) He covers the same distance, hopping first on the right foot then the left
   - c) He jumps, feet together, along the line.

   Observe carefully during these exercises the position of the child's arms and hands. The purpose of the activity is to restrict the associated movements so if the other limbs are waving around the body involuntarily, give the child something to hold, heavy enough to bring his hands down by his side. Then gradually reduce the weight until the arms and hands become naturally relaxed on each side of the body.

   If only one hand/arm is affected use weights only on that side.

3. **Measured crawl**

   It is important that the child is able to use arms and legs independently from each other. This is a difficult task for youngsters to master if they have not gone through the crawling stage as babies. After demonstration, use a variety of heights and textures to crawl over.

Fig 5:5 Course layout

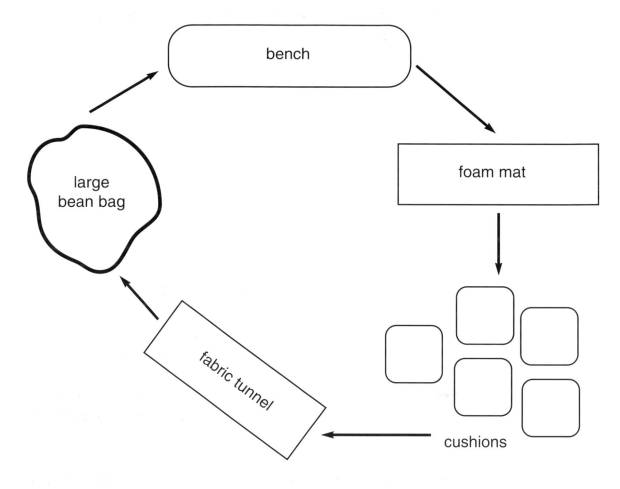

4. **Bean bags** - measure distance and target.

   Bean bags have an advantage over small tennis balls in that they do not bounce and the session is not spent chasing them.

   The child should be positioned from the target so that he can achieve a 4/10 success: 2 metres is the usual starting distance when aiming at a target 1/2 metre square. As the child becomes more skilful, increase the distance. Assess the success in 10 tries for:

   a) Both hands
   b) Right hand
   c) Left hand.

   Assess associated movements: if the child is unable to stand still while throwing he could place his feet under the lower frame of a bench. If the left hand is waving while the right is throwing use weights to bring the arm down.

5. Large ball play

As before, ensure the child stands a measured distance from the target and record success in 10 tries for:

   a) Both hands
   b) Right hand
   c) Left hand.

Check for associated movements.

6. Skateboard

Use a measured line between 7 and 10 metres in length.

Ask the child to propel himself, using only his arms, forwards and backwards along the measured line. The position should be:

   a) Long sitting, facing forwards with legs out in front
   b) Low kneeling, on both heels and balancing on the board.

Each child was given the programme shown in Figure 5:5 adjusted weekly as skills were achieved. The record chart was marked each day the child accessed the programme and progress was measured every Friday.

Figure 5:6 shows a completed activity chart dated April 1994. The programme has been extended to reflect the pupil's developing skills.

The sequence of activities and how to determine those most suitable for individual children is detailed in chapters 6 and 7.

In June the pupils were re-assessed and their achievements discussed with parents. After the intervention 7 of the youngsters in the study had developed motor skills which were well within the average range expected for pupils of their age. The pupils, parents and teachers were asked to comment on the effectiveness of the programmes. Samples of pupils' work illustrate some of the changes: Figures 5:7, 5:8, 5:9.

Fig 5:6

Record Sheet

Date............

ACTIVITY	BASELINE BEHAVIOUR	PROGRAMME DURATION										TARGETS	ACHIEVED Y/N
		3/5	4/5	5/5	6/5	9/5	10/5	11/5	12/5	13/5	14/5		
Measured line jumping two feet together (time taken in seconds)	absent 29.4.94 not tested	✓	✓	✓	4	✓	✓	✓	✓	6	✓	8	N
Jumping, two feet together, over turning skipping rope (Nos in 60 secs)		✓	✓	✓	6	✓	✓	✓	✓	24	✓	20	Y
Clapping 1 - 2,3,4 (Nos in 30 secs)		✓	✓	✓	10	✓	✓	✓	✓	12	✓	15	N
Large ball, single bounce and catch (Nos in 30 secs)		✓	✓	✓	8	✓	✓	✓	✓	8	✓	10	N
Small ball, single bounce and catch (Nos in 30 secs)		✓	✓	✓	6	✓	✓	✓	✓	16	✓	15	Y
Skateboard low kneel both hands working together (4m)		✓	✓	✓	13	✓	✓	✓	✓	18	✓	15	Y
Long sitting 5 objects either side 10 times (6 to cross mid line)		✓	✓	✓	3	✓	✓	✓	✓	7	✓	10	N

April 1994

Fig 5:7 Pupil X

Writing sample from September 1993

> Monday september
> 6th I went on my
> holidays and I went
> fishing.

Writing sample from November 1993

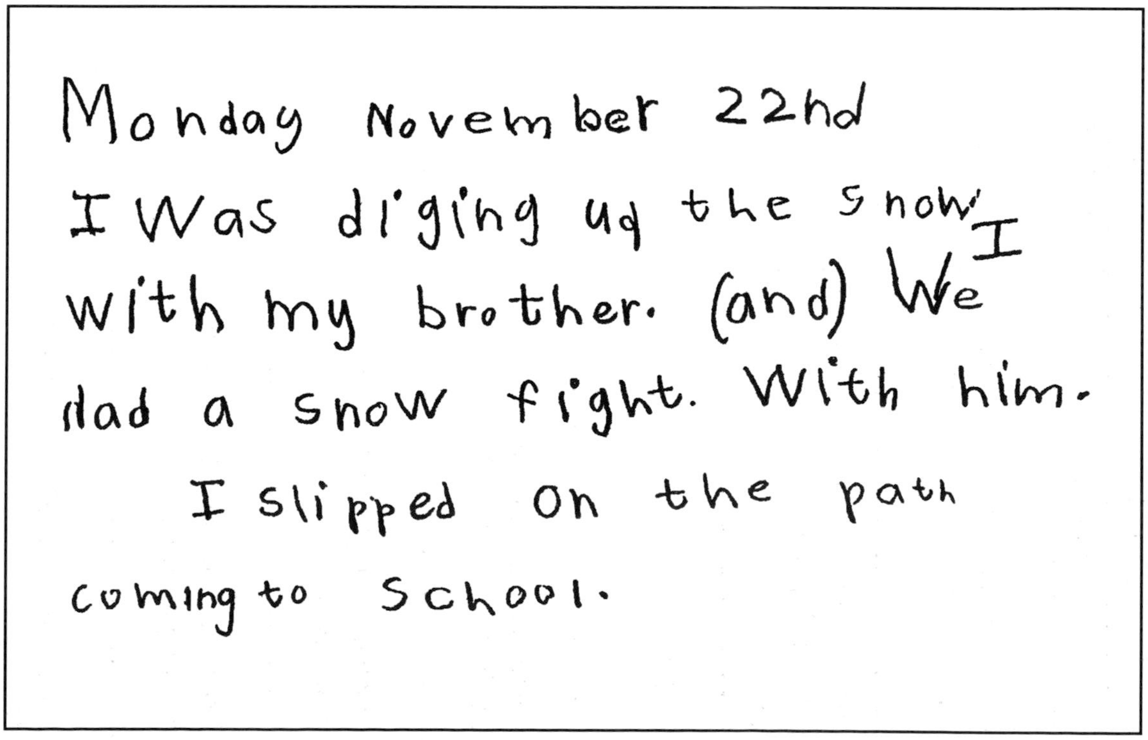

> Monday November 22nd
> I Was diging up the snow
> with my brother. (and) We I
> dad a snow fight. With him.
>   I slipped On the path
> coming to School.

Fig. 5:8 Pupil Y

Writing sample from September 1993

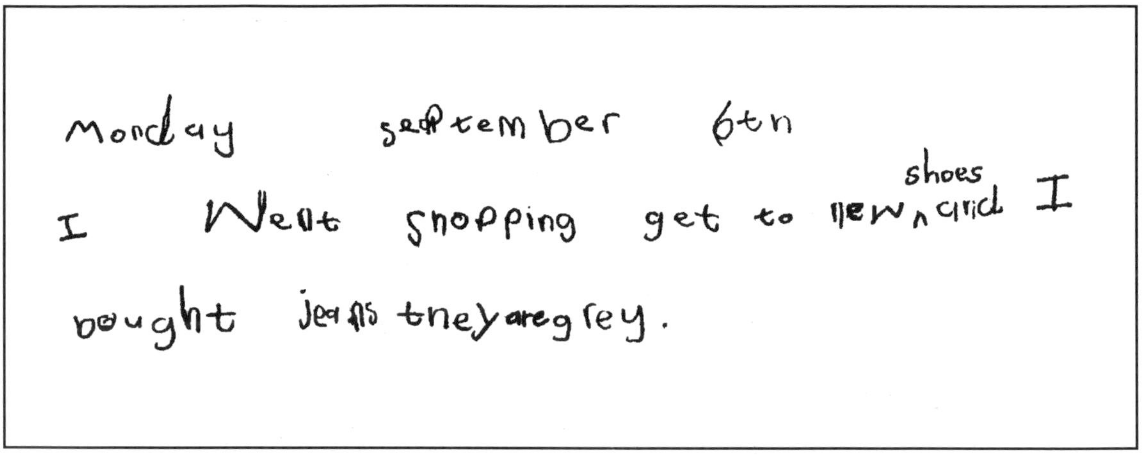

Monday   september   6th
I   Went   snopping   get   to   new shoes and   I
bought   jeans theyaregrey.

Writing sample from January 1994

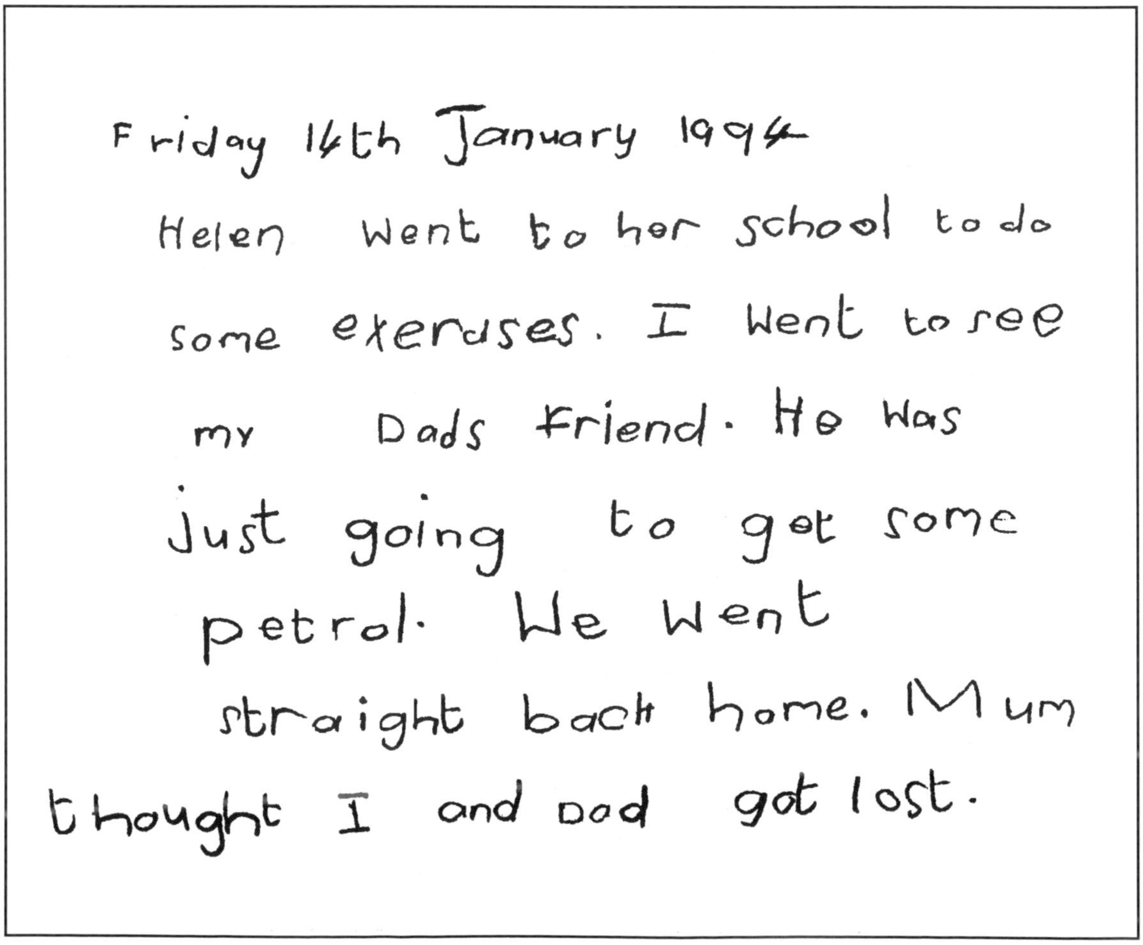

Friday 16th January 1994
    Helen   Went   to her   school   to do
    some   exeruses.   I   Went   to see
    my   Dads   friend.   He   Was
    Just   going   to   get   some
    petrol.   We   Went
        straight   back   home.   Mum
thought   I   and   Dad   got lost.

Fig. 5:9 Pupil Z

Number work from September 1993

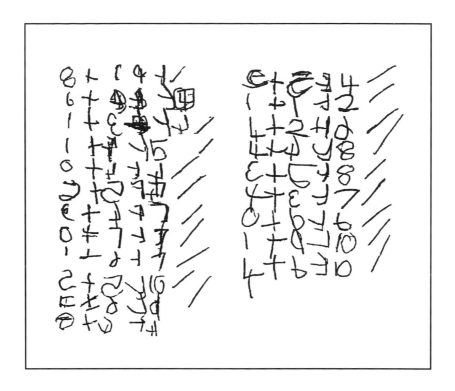

Number work from January 1994

Developmental
— Dyspraxia

Thomas - a case study

Thomas was referred for assessment when he was 6. He had transferred to a primary school in the county at 5½ years and was admitted into the reception class.

Thomas had found it very difficult to relate appropriately to the other pupils. He had speech and language difficulties and he often attempted to make contact using physical gestures. He was viewed by the children as rough and at times aggressive. His class-teacher was most concerned about his very limited concentration and poor fine motor skills. After a term in his new school, parents and staff believed that a detailed assessment of his behaviour was necessary to provide a baseline for an individual education programme.

A meeting with parents revealed that there had been difficulties from birth. He was premature and his mother had gone into labour at 35 weeks. There were signs of foetal distress during the second stage and Thomas was born by emergency caesarean section. "He cried constantly during the first 6 months". A variety of milk-based and substitute products had been tried with little success. Weight gain had been poor and at 8 months he was admitted to hospital for observation because of his failure to thrive.

Largely the crying ceased at 10 months but he always appeared to be insecure. Mother said that until starting nursery she had to take him with her even when going to the toilet.

Thomas was able to sit independently at 9 months and began to 'bottom shuffle' at 13 months. He could pull himself to a standing position at 18 months and walked independently at 22/23 months.

There had been some concerns at the 18-month check because Thomas was able to drink only from a feeder cup and was making no attempt to use a spoon appropriately. He was making some babbling sounds but was unable to say any recognisable words. Referral was made to the speech therapy service and he was assessed at 2½ years.

Between the ages of 2 and 3 Thomas had uncontrolled tantrums, screaming and kicking and sometimes banging his head on the floor. When Thomas was 3 years 2 months his sister Helen arrived. At the same time, Dad was made redundant and could only find work abroad. The next 6 months Mum said were the worst time of her life. Thomas, who could never be described as a good sleeper, was waking even more frequently (6/7 times during the night). He was aggressive towards his younger sister and he would become very easily distressed about nothing. One example was when he had been given a chocolate bar to eat and when the wrapper was opened it had broken into two pieces. Thomas's response was one of 'hysteria' which continued for almost an hour.

At the age of 3½ Thomas was placed in a pre-school language unit every morning and attended weekly sessions at the Department of Child and Family Psychiatry. Sibling rivalry and the absence for long periods of a father who had previously been very involved with his son were, perhaps understandably, thought to have been the explanation for Thomas's difficulties.

Although there was a significant improvement in Thomas's speech during the next 12 months there was little change in his behaviour. Mum, by then, found Thomas so difficult that she felt she could no longer manage on her own. Dad gave up his job and returned home. It had been expected that this would effect a change in Thomas's behaviour. None was observed. The problems remained unresolved and 12 months later Dad found new employment and the family moved. Thomas was referred to me a term later.

Thomas had a very immature pencil grip and he found it very difficult to co-ordinate movement in his hand. Colouring and copying skills were approximately 2 years delayed and he had very limited perception of objects in space. He ran with an awkward gait with his hands moving wildly in the air. Gross motor skills were similarly delayed. Thomas was unable to write his name unaided and his copy-writing was indecipherable, but his understanding of mathematical concepts was age-appropriate. He could add 11 + 7 and verbally give the right answer. He could not write it down. Assessment using the WPPSI confirmed that his general knowledge and comprehension skills were also age-appropriate although some of his words were indistinct.

Thomas's developmental and cognitive profiles confirmed that he was dyspraxic. His working day was broken down into shorter periods and the amount of manual recording required from him was reduced by 50%. For Thomas it was his parents' greater understanding of his difficulties which brought about the most significant changes. Instead of giving him a string of instructions he was asked to do one thing at a time. This meant he could actually remember what he was doing. Work at school was now completed so he no longer spent playtime finishing off. He began an exercise programme with two other pupils with similar, although less severe difficulties. The three boys started to develop a close friendships and they called for each other at the weekend.

Thomas continued to have problems with concentration, but because he was allowed to move to another activity after 10 minutes in a 60-minute session he was on task for between 45 and 50 minutes. If, instead, he had had access to only 2 activities each of 20 minutes duration he would have achieved a maximum of 20 minutes on task during the hour session

There are increasing numbers of youngsters who are now being diagnosed as dyspraxic. While there are many behaviours which are consistent among the majority, each child must have an individual programme of work which emphasises his strengths and consequently gives him sufficient confidence and raised self-esteem to attempt to progress in areas he finds extremely difficult.

Chapter
6

Remediation programmes
for the "early years"

*B*y the time dyspraxic children are 3, many symptoms of the condition may be apparent. There will be some evidence of the delayed acquisition of motor skills and in addition there may be language difficulties. Chapter 3 outlined specific targets for achievement and the aim now is to look at programmes to ameliorate the difficulties experienced by dyspraxic children. Skills are usually acquired in a particular sequence so, if we establish a baseline for the child's ability in all areas of development we can specify the next target. For example, the child requires a good pincer grasp to be able to complete inset boards competently, so appropriate activities to develop the skill should be devised. The programmes which follow identify sequentially the developmental targets and suggest methods of teaching the skills.

Social skills

Dressing: *This can be a nightmare which continues well into secondary education if a routine is not established at an early age*

Encourage the child to hold his arms and legs in the correct position for the removal and putting on of jumper and trousers.

As this is achieved let the child pull off his own socks. Start with the sock halfway off the foot and then allow the child to remove it. Gradually reduce assistance until he can manage unaided.

Similarly, teach the child to put on his socks, beginning by pulling the leg just past the ankle. Move it farther down the foot until he can eventually manage himself.

Trousers can be mastered if at first the child is required only to pull them up from his knees. Progress to ankles and then teach the child how to place legs in separately. By giving the child the easy part of the task to learn first, he will be encouraged to keep trying. This technique can be adopted for all articles of clothing.

Try to choose shoes with Velcro fasteners if you expect the child to have increasing success at this age. Fastening laces and buckles are separate skills to master.

Feeding: *Manipulating just a spoon to the mouth may require a great deal of practice. Very young dyspraxic children find it almost impossible to co-ordinate two feeding implements*

Up to the age of 3 encourage the child to feed with just a spoon or fork. Ensure that there is sufficient food on the plate so the child is not trying to co-ordinate his movements to stab one pea. Cut food to the correct size for eating and, during the early stages, place your hand on top of the child's to steady the movement from the plate to the mouth. As the child becomes more competent move your hand to his elbow reducing the level of help required. The child will become confident only if he has had success while trying to acquire the new skill. If the task has been too difficult from the outset he will become easily frustrated and refuse even to pick up a fork or spoon.

Drinking: *Changing from a bottle to a handled cup and then a beaker presents great difficulties*

Follow the same routine as for feeding. Give the child a two-handled cup and steady the base while the child brings it to his mouth. Again, gradually reduce your assistance and move slowly to a one- handled cup and then a beaker. The consumption of food continues to present difficulties for the dyspraxic child, often into secondary education. If these skills can be taught at an early stage a great deal of embarrassment will be avoided.

Sleeping: *Often patterns established during the first 6 - 12 months which may have been the result of severe colic or milk intolerance are extremely difficult to change*

The child may be having 8 - 10 hours sleep each day but this may be split into many cat-naps. Discourage sleeping during the day if possible and this may enable some of the brief periods of sleeping to merge. Once the child starts to settle for 5+ hours reduce further sleeping outside this time and ensure that he is active during the day so he is more likely to be tired at bedtime. Some children continue to be very restless even when they are able to sleep for longer periods and parents report that this unsettled behaviour can become a part of the dyspraxic child's routine.

Relationships with other children: *Language plays an important part in communicating with others. The dyspraxic child may be severely disadvantaged*

Encourage the child to become involved in games which develop co-operative play. It is important that an adult is present to organise the activity. The dyspraxic child imitates others at play and copies rather than co-operates. Defined activities are much easier for him to understand: for example to play on a see-saw requires the two children to work co-operatively. Turn-taking is a problem and it is important that they are encouraged to wait until the toys are available rather than physically remove the object from another child.

Toilet training: *The child, apart from understanding when it is appropriate to use the toilet, has to learn to remove his clothes appropriately*

Once the child recognises the physical symptoms which indicate the need to use the toilet, try to make it as easy as possible to achieve success. Choose clothes with elasticated waists so trousers can be removed easily. The child must feel secure while using the toilet and steps must be taken to compensate for the problems with balance experienced by dyspraxic youngsters. It is helpful to place a small box next to the toilet for the child to rest his feet. If the legs are left swinging the child will spend more time establishing a secure seating position than using the toilet appropriately.

Behaviour: *The dyspraxic child can become easily frustrated but it is important to decide how much of the difficult behaviour is directly related to the condition*

Sometimes the 'label' can be used as an excuse for a whole range of difficulties, behaviour to name but one. If the child is unable to complete a task or cannot comprehend the instructions given then we may excuse the inappropriate behaviour which is a direct consequence of his frustration. If the child merely wants his own way or responds aggressively towards another pupil, this is not acceptable and strategies to impose discipline should be employed. Parents know when their child is likely to become provoked. Try to avoid the escalation of any situation which will result in distress. If a task is too difficult, distract him with an alternative. Give clear instructions so that the child knows exactly what is expected. Always be consistent in your own behaviour: if the child's behaviour is unacceptable always reaffirm the consequences.

Language development

A speech therapist may already be involved and will provide specific programmes to follow

If there are general concerns about language development involve the child in games and exercises which use and strengthen the facial muscles. Make faces and ask the child to copy. Blowing bubbles is always popular and it encourages the movement of the lips and the control of breathing. When the child begins to make sounds use them to devise single words. If he can say "b" choose words which begin with b - ball, bag, bat, and reinforce the word with the real object at first, then move to pictures. As concentration is a problem the child is more likely to retain his interest in the discussion if a real toy is present. The young child finds it difficult to process large amounts of verbal information so keep instructions short and limit sentences to as few words as possible like: "Point to the ball". Repeat sentences in the same form and encourage the child to listen to and repeat nursery rhymes.

Motor skills

During the early stages of development it is the execution of motor skills which encourages the development of the neural pathways in the brain. It is having access to motor skills programmes which is fundamental to the remediation of dyspraxia and this is paramount, irrespective of the age of the child. Dyspraxic children find it extremely difficult to execute tasks which involve co-ordination of arms and legs and whereas the majority of youngsters acquire naturally a level of ability in such activities, the dyspraxic child can do so only with practice.

Some parents have said to me: "He couldn't possibly be dyspraxic, he plays football for the school team". The child has practised a particular skill to a level which is more than competent. However, with dyspraxic youngsters these skills do not generalise to other areas and in the case of the good footballers they had very poor co-ordination of their upper limb movements. Because these skills are not acquired naturally each has to be taught separately to the child. This can be compared with some children who experience difficulties with reading. They may recognise letter sounds but are unable to prefix them to blends. For example, the word ending could be *at*. With different initial letters the word could be read as:

> m*at*
> s*at*
> c*at*
> b*at*
> h*at*

The child who is unable to generalise the sound *at* cannot merely prefix the different letters but has to learn 5 separate words.

If the child cannot generalise newly-acquired movements, each activity has to be broken down into its components and taught sequentially. This is the purpose of directing the child to specific motor activities.

At the pre-school stage (under 3) many parents believe that they are unsupported in working through their child's difficulties. As with older pupils, rate of progress is much faster when the remediation programme is carried out with the support of other children and familiar adults. This can be the case for the younger child if he has access to structured movement activities outside the home but within the local community. The dyspraxic child will benefit most from the structured sessions because given the freedom to choose the activity it would not be one which involved much co-ordination of motor skills. Play-groups are important to encourage development of the child's inter-personal skills but in addition the dyspraxic child should have the facility to learn to climb and co-ordinate movements on pieces of large apparatus.

The Tumble Tots programme is one I have studied and would recommend to parents concerned about a child experiencing difficulties with the acquisition of motor skills. Classes are organised for children up to the age of 7.

The idea for establishing such provision originated when Bill Cosgrave, an Olympic gymnastics coach, began working with youngsters in schools in 1979. He believes that physical skills have to be learned; they are not inherited. He has devised programmes which teach the components of basic motor skills in an enjoyable and child-centred environment.

The schemes are well structured and run by trained, qualified members of staff. Although the programmes are designed to benefit all children under 7, the organisation has recognised the importance of extending the provision to include youngsters with special educational needs. The leaders' handbook makes particular reference to youngsters with perceptual motor difficulties and highlights the organisation's awareness of the condition. It suggests that symptoms exist in varying degrees and are compounded by frustration, low self-esteem, lack of patience and repeated failures. The following directions are given to instructors:

● children will respond to tasks which are appropriate for their level of ability

● effort and success must be recognised and praise should be constant

● tasks requiring balance, rhythm and co-ordination are most useful Both gross and fine motor skills will require breaking down into the most simple stages of progression

● spatial and perceptual difficulties are evident and these may be signs of poor motor organisation

● ball handling skills will be difficult to achieve and careful attention to the correct sequencing is essential for progress.

Motor skills programmes encourage children to develop their abilities progressively. Parents are involved from the outset to ensure that there is the opportunity to practise newly-acquired and emerging skills at home. This is an integral part of the programme as children with motor difficulties need more time to learn to co-ordinate movements.

Sessions are divided so that time can be given to the child working individually with large apparatus and part can be spent in the group working co-operatively, manipulating a large parachute or responding with appropriate gestures to nursery rhymes. Examples of some of the equipment and its function are:

1. *Meccano walking*

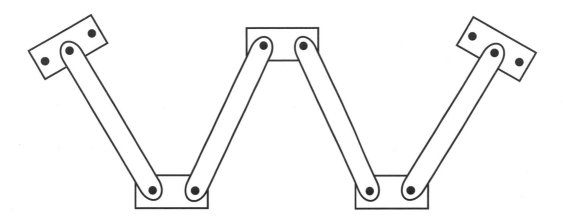

Apparatus which develops balance and gross motor co-ordination skills. It has a 4 inch walking surface 3 inches off the ground, allowing a wide range of shapes to be presented. Children are encouraged to walk along the beams, arms outstretched.

2. *Wobble boards*

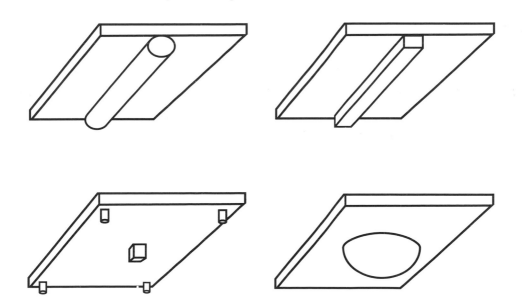

This apparatus helps the child to determine the centre of gravity in his body. It develops the ability to maintain balance forward, backward and left to right. A variety of boards offer different surface angles.

3. Box tunnel

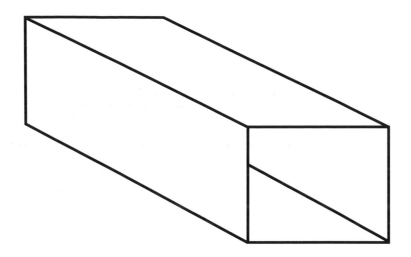

The tunnel is designed for the early toddler and incorporates two different heights. The child is encouraged to improve his crawling ability and move his limbs in a co-ordinated manner.

4. Spring ball

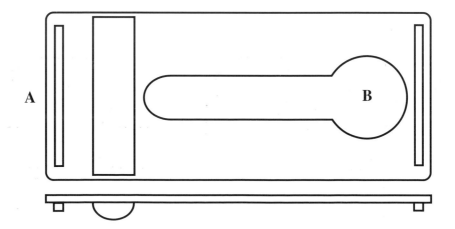

Appropriate for the development of good eye-hand and eye-foot co-ordination for all ages. A small sponge ball is placed at point B and pressure applied at point A with hand or foot launches the ball into the air.

5. *Bird beam*

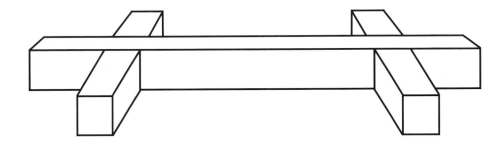

A long wooden beam for low balance and locomotor activities.   Comprises an interchangeable 4" and 2" walking surface.

6. *Stepping stones*

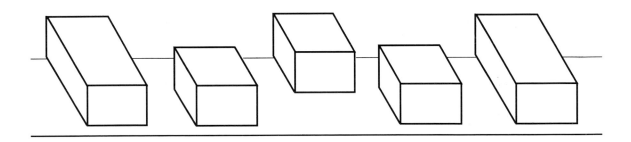

The child is encouraged to place one foot on each step and the activity is designed to develop eye-foot co-ordination. Body awareness of right and left is also extended.

— Dyspraxia

As the child becomes more familiar with the activity let him hold a bean bag* or soft toy in each hand. With improving confidence he will be able to balance without touching anything. If the child is able to achieve 5+ seconds on each foot by the age of 4 this is an acceptable standard.

Continue to develop the child's skills by encouraging him to balance on a variety of textures, e.g. sand, foam mat or cushions.

By the age of 3 the majority of youngsters will be able to pedal a trike. This is not the case with dyspraxic children. They find it difficult enough co-ordinating the pedals without trying to steer as well. Unfortunately the trike usually has the pedals on the front wheel, which requires far greater effort to execute the turning movement. It is much easier when the child is 4 - 5 and can sit astride a bike with stabilisers. The pedals are directly below the line of the body and the larger wheels require less force to make the turning arc. The dyspraxic child may find it impossible to master the skills required to ride the smaller trike so it may be less distressing if he uses a 'sit-astride trike'* and waits until he is tall enough for the larger model. (The sit-astride trike does not have any pedals and the child propels himself using his feet. It is very similar in design to the trikes other children the same age would be using).

Fine motor skills

From an early age, the dyspraxic child avoids tasks which require good manipulative skills. This is unfortunate because the configuring of smaller pieces into larger shapes (Lego and Meccano) and the completion of jigsaws and inset puzzles are the foundation for the development of good perceptual skills. As it is the motor component of the task which is discouraging it is important to offer alternatives to the usual 'play' equipment of young children. The larger plastic pieces such as Mega Blocks* and Waffle* make construction tasks much easier. In addition, give the child inset boards with large handles* attached to the pieces. This enables him to develop knowledge about shapes without relying on a good pincer grasp to complete the activity.

Ability to co-ordinate eye-hand movement is another emerging skill which needs to be extended. Although it would be expected that by the age of 3 a child should be threading beads and buttons, the dyspraxic child is often not able to manipulate the materials adequately and becomes very frustrated if asked to do so. There are far more interesting threading activities available which do not involve such small pieces of equipment. Suggestions would be 'Threading fruit; Threading butterfly'* and the 'Lacing shoe'*. The magnetic fish game is always popular with young children and there is a delightful extension of this called 'Foam fishing'* using large fish and it can be played in the bath. Any activity should be regarded as fun to complete or the child will be reluctant to perform the task.

Another activity which improves perceptual skills and develops eye-hand co-ordination is the moulding of clay and dough into recognisable shapes. This encourages the development of tactile skills which are often immature in dyspraxic children. Roll shapes like snakes so the child experiences the texture of the material in his hands. Shape cutters provide good templates for directed activities.

The programmes developed for the pre-school child are extended into the nursery environment where the child should be given as many opportunities as possible to improve his skills.

Activities in the nursery

Observing the dyspraxic child in the nursery gives parents and staff the opportunity to record the activities generally enjoyed and those which are avoided. His ability to concentrate, his language skills and the relationships with other children are important details of baseline behaviour.

Because the dyspraxic youngster has difficulty understanding the concept of time the day requires some structure, and a method of indicating to the child what is going to happen next should be established. He needs access to a visually structured environment as verbal instructions are difficult to process. When giving information always use clear language and remember that dyspraxic pupils have problems separating relevant information from background noise. An example of the type of instruction which might be used at the end of the session is: "Tidy-up time". The child should be established in a routine where he knows the procedure when that announcement is made. It is much more relevant to him than saying: "Now I would like you all to stop what you are doing and clear the tables ready for story-time". In the example 3 words convey the same meaning as 20.

Initially the dyspraxic child may find it very difficult to settle down and may be observed moving quickly between activities. Water play and sand are relatively secure and will not usually present any difficulties. The construction table will be visited infrequently, often to knock down rather than build up designs. The drawing table will be avoided, although when pushed he will make a few scribbled marks on the paper. Depending on the nature of the activities outdoor play can present an excellent means of extending gross motor skills.

Nursery environment

● use black line drawings on card to identify areas of activity (see Appendix A). Attach the card next to the water play, home corner, computer etc. and keep a separate set of cards for use with the child

- ensure that the child knows what is expected of him. Demonstrate activity first

- provide structure for the child so that he knows, for example, that the session begins when he removes his coat, is halfway through at snack time and ends with story or nursery-rhymes

- ensure that when seated the chair is the appropriate height for the table.

Extension activities

Fine motor skills

Begin by encouraging the child to make shapes* and patterns in the sand or spray foam using his fingers.

Develop the child's understanding of textures using a 'feelie bag' and tactile touch cards*.

Make shapes from clay, sand and play dough. Start using animal or shape cutters*.

Give the child access to screw toys to develop fine prehension and wrist movements. Appropriate activities would be Geo nuts and bolts*.

Encourage the child to develop 'cutting' skills, perhaps in the life area with plastic fruit* or bread* where the slices are attached by Velcro.

As described in the pre-school programme, the dyspraxic child will have difficulty threading beads so access to large pieces of equipment like the lacing shoe* or the butterfly* will enable him to master the skill.

The dyspraxic child needs encouragement to develop pre-writing skills and the activities should be broken into small steps. Initially, direct the child to the painting corner and begin with fingers and hands. When the child is able to hold the brush appropriately encourage him to make large arcs and circles on the paper. After developing circular motion allow the child to copy vertical and horizontal lines.

When the child is ready to use crayons and pencils he may find the 'chubbi-stumps' difficult to manipulate and prefer to use felt-tips or ordinary pencils. If pencil grip continues to be weak allow the child to use those which are triangular* in shape.

Closing scissors can be extremely frustrating and a suggestion would be to use Stirex* scissors which are manipulated by squeezing the whole hand. The child may then have success with self-opening scissors* which accommodate youngsters with a weak grip. If the whole idea is too difficult it is possible to obtain double-handed training scissors*.

Perceptual skills

As the child develops his fine motor skills he will be able to complete a range of tasks which extend his perceptual ability. A specially-designed weaving loom* develops good manipulative skills and the child has the incentive to produce a sample which can be converted into a scarf or table mat.

Reproducing shapes either by drawing or building should be extended. Again access to large apparatus Waffle* and Mega Blocks* should be offered instead of the more usual nursery equipment like Lego. Templates* can be used but the dyspraxic child who has problems crossing the mid-line of his body may copy around the right side with his right hand and change to his left hand to finish it off. When hand-dominance is established demonstrate to the child how the shape can be drawn using one hand.

The dyspraxic child has problems co-ordinating both hands and forgets to secure the paper with one hand while drawing with the other. Use Blu-tack or paper clips to keep the paper in place.

Problems with manipulative skills will discourage the child from attempting jigsaws and formboards. There are many age-appropriate inset boards* available which have large handles attached to the pieces.

Encourage the child to work on sequencing tasks which may be to order 3 pictures to make sense of a story or to arrange shapes ▲ ▲ ▲ in order of size. Magnetic boards* and Fuzzy-felt shapes overcome the problems of drawing.

Language development and social skills

A child with verbal dyspraxia may have good understanding but limited communication skills. Nursery children show acceptance of other pupils with speech difficulties. The child will become anxious and frustrated if he cannot communicate his ideas. Follow the child's gestures and use the symbol cards to change activity.

The dyspraxic child may prefer to be on his own so initially he should be encouraged to work alongside and then with another pupil. This environment will have to be created because the other pupils may find his excitable behaviour difficult to accept.

—Dyspraxia

Poor attentional skills are characteristic and a personal target may be set initially for the child to spend 5 minutes on each activity. This should be extended as appropriate.

The dyspraxic child finds imaginative play difficult to comprehend but with the help of an adult can learn to relate. Dressing up and playing different roles involves the child with other pupils.

Information conveyed verbally can be very confusing and story-time may present problems. The child is unable to concentrate and sit still for periods in excess of a few minutes and arrangements should be made to accommodate this difficulty. Perhaps he could be allowed to turn the pages and point to the pictures. He may be required to join the group for only the last 5 minutes, gradually extending the time as his concentration improves.

Gross motor activities

Motor activities can be structured to produce particular movements, for example when copying the appropriate actions in nursery rhymes. The dyspraxic child takes longer to process information and will perform the actions after the other children. Make sure that an adult is available to help the child to sequence his motor movements in time, and with repetition he will master the task. If support is not in place at the outset he will be aware quickly that he cannot achieve the desired response and will become distressed.

Climbing, running and playing on large play equipment should be encouraged. Access to specific pieces of equipment like play cubes* and tunnels* develops movement skills frequently by-passed in the early years. Balance beams* and wobble boards*, as described previously, extend the child's skills. Parents may encourage their child to attend out-of-school gymnastics sessions.

Additional information

The child must enjoy going to nursery and incentives are necessary to encourage him to attempt tasks he finds difficult. A personal chart* in the nursery and at home is a record of his achievements. Stars and stickers are visible rewards and are a recognition of his effort. The following is an example of a possible chart:

Child X has been attending nursery during the morning sessions for 6 weeks. He loves using the computer and playing outdoors in the sandpit but has difficulty relating to other pupils and refuses to enter the story corner at the end of the session. In addition his fine motor skills are immature but he is able to scribble with crayons on a piece of paper.

Target behaviour for X

Long-term goals:

1. To work co-operatively with another pupil for 5 minutes

2. To sit appropriately through story time for 15 minutes

3. To copy unaided a ●, ■ and ▲ using a pencil.

The programme must develop X's skills to achieve the long-term goals and offer rewards to encourage him to perform the specified activities.

Symbols on the chart refer to these activities which in detail are:

On arrival at nursery X will be allowed to use the computer by himself for 10 minutes

Still sitting at the computer X will play co-operatively with another child

Developmental Dyspraxia

X will sit for 3 minutes at the snack table

X can play in the sand or water until story-time

X will sit next to the teacher and hold the story book for 2 minutes and then be allowed to return to the computer

Fig: 6:1

— Dyspraxia

The child can mark the chart himself each day to record his progress (Figure 6:1). The co-operative play may change and the time spent in story-time can be extended until X's behaviour is appropriate by comparison to the rest of the group. It is not necessary continually to monitor 5 activities; choose the number appropriate for the child.

Always break the task down into smaller steps to enable to child to achieve success. Use zips and Velcro fasteners instead of buttons and laces if possible, and if problems persist when the child is trying to co-ordinate a knife and fork use angled cutlery* until he is able to effect more accurate control.

Activities for children in the reception class

On transfer to reception the child will be aware of the change in the classroom environment. The curriculum is more formal and there is reduced opportunity for the child to improve his gross motor skills. Outside play is available only at the prescribed time. Organised games and access to specialised equipment is usually restricted to PE lessons, although some schools provide fixed outdoor climbing frames and have permanent markings on the playground for games such as hop-scotch. The dyspraxic child will be able to avoid activities essential for development if he is not directed towards them.

Integration of the child within his peer group should be established as soon as possible because this is the most significant factor in ensuring future progress and happiness in school. Children who experience rejection from an early stage in school often become isolated, have low self-esteem and exhibit extreme behavioural difficulties before reaching the end of their primary education. Initially relationships within the classroom may have to be engineered until the other children are able to understand the difficulties experienced by the dyspraxic child. Many teachers express concerns about identifying the problems with some pupils and discussing them with the whole group. Children are very observant and know when another pupil is finding some of the work difficult. By saying nothing, the less able child will become the victim of comment and criticism. A more positive ethos is achieved when the whole class is involved in offering support as highlighted in the previous chapter.

It is important that parents and staff are involved in planning activities for the child to ensure that approaches are consistent at home and in school.

Classroom environment
● provide structure to the day and establish routines for entering and leaving the classroom

- position the child centrally in the classroom where he cannot touch wall displays or equipment either in cupboards or on tables

- ensure that eye contact is made with the child before giving instructions

- keep verbal information succinct when directing an activity and use visual clues whenever possible

- be prepared to modify the task: if there is a motor skill component allow extra time

- classroom furniture should be sturdy and secure - dyspraxic children have poor stability.

Extension activities

Gross motor skills

The structured programmes offered by specialist outside agencies are ideal for the child at this stage. Activities are developed by qualified instructors and the child will have access to equipment designed to improve balance, co-ordination and perceptual skills. Parents can continue the recommended exercises during the week as the dyspraxic child requires more practice to acquire the skill. Whether the activities are to be carried out in school, at home or with other specialist tutors the programme should include:

- balancing on each foot, extending activity to different surfaces and wobble boards*

- walking heel to toe along a small beam or painted line

- jumping, feet together - a trampoline will make the task more enjoyable

- hopping a distance of up to 4 metres

- climbing ladders and steps - hand and feet moving in opposition

- crawling on all fours - an activity tunnel* provides greater incentive

- kicking a ball towards a 1 metre target placed 4 metres from the child

- running a measured distance of 10+ metres.

— Dyspraxia

Observe the child's hand movements during these activities. The purpose is not only to acquire the skills to be able to hop, jump etc. but to separate out the associated hand movements. If arms and hands are flailing around give the child an object to hold. A large sponge ball held with both hands prevents involuntary hand movements and enables the child to achieve better posture and master the skill. Keep practising the activity in this manner until the associated movements cease and then proceed without holding the ball. To achieve the balancing skills the child should complete the activities with his arms outstretched. It may help to hold a bean bag* in each hand.

A programme to develop co-ordinated upper body movement should include:

● throwing and catching a large ball a distance of 3 metres

● target practice - large ball aimed with both hands at a 50cm target 3 metres away

● wheelbarrow game - hold the legs of the child, initially at the knees then ankles, as he develops the skills of walking forwards on his hands

● hedgehog balls* are very stimulating and can be used for massage and finger exercises.

Fine motor skills

By the time the child enters the reception class he will be expected to have developed many pre-writing skills. This depends on the child's ability to interpret what he is seeing and have sufficiently mature fine motor co-ordination to reproduce it. Some of the activities suggested for nursery age children may be appropriate initially for pupils of school age. When the child is able to hold a crayon or pencil and can use scissors, even with some residual difficulty, it is important that attention is focused on the development of his handwriting. The ability to write legibly is a skill which must be taught as it is not simply acquired. The majority of dyspraxic children who, even by the age of 13 and 14 still cannot produce anything on paper which can be readily interpreted, have developed a poor handwriting style. At the outset this was based on incorrect letter formation and a limited conceptual awareness of page layout. As the child progresses through the education system he is required manually to record increasing quantities of information. The quality of that recording can be viewed as a reflection of the child's ability. Dyspraxic children can easily be judged as failing if handwriting is a factor in the assessment. The child will benefit greatly from adopting the correct style in the beginning. Such children are very good at developing their own unsatisfactory compensatory system.

Provide the child with a writing implement which is comfortable to use. Dyspraxic children often have a weak grip and consequently over-compensate by holding the pencil too tightly. The result will be a broken point or a torn page.

A triangular pencil or triangular grip will help the child establish the correct finger positions. Grips with animal shapes* attached are very popular with younger children and are available from the Early Learning Centre. Parents may find it helpful to encourage the child to use the same aids at home.

Encourage the child to colour simple pictures and shapes. Felt-tipped pens require less pressure and produce more colourful results than pencils or crayons. Develop left-right orientation and mark the starting point on the page. Pre-writing skills worksheets* provide a series of graded exercises which encourage left-to-right tracking skills and basic letter patterns. To complement this programme the child would benefit from the Rol'n'Write* scheme which involves a steel ball slowly tracing the letter in the correct sequence. In addition the child can follow the groove with his finger. The exercise develops fine motor control and improves fluency of letter formation.

The dyspraxic child finds it almost impossible to record sequentially on a blank page. Draw lines and mark the left side of the page with a dot. Allow the youngster to explore the shape of letters before attempting to copy them. When an understanding of the letter shape is achieved the child should be shown how to produce the appropriate size. Typically, dyspraxic children will produce script which is a mixture of upper and lower case letters of varying heights with no spaces between the words. They continue to be unaware of the rules of writing unless repeatedly pointed out to them. N.E.S. Arnold has produced a selection of 26 templates which incorporate a series of graded letter grooves. As the letter size decreases the children acquire more controlled handwriting skills and are able to form the correct appropriately sized shapes.

Handwriting is a major part of the classroom curriculum and there are many activities which encourage the development of the fine motor skills required to produce correctly formed letters. Flexibility of the wrist can be improved if the child is encouraged to make continuous large circular patterns with a paint brush. Attach the paper to an easel as the skill can be mastered quickly on a vertical rather than a flat surface. The Ayres Collection has developed a series of wooden panels with cut out tracks which become increasingly complex. The target is to pull the bead along the pre-determined track.

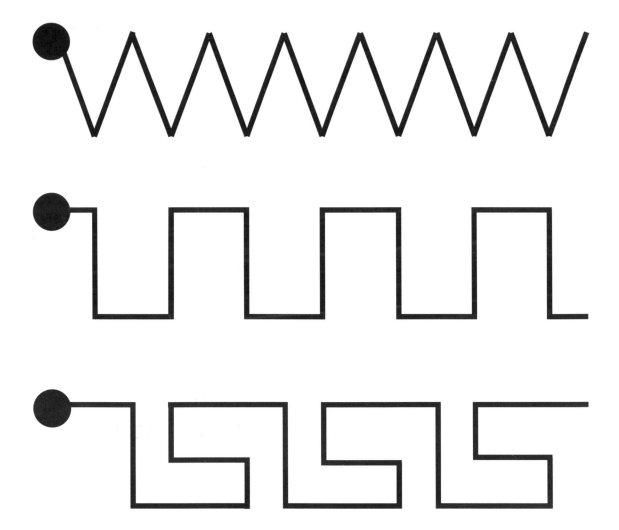

As the child becomes more confident with pencil control he will enjoy completing simple dot-to-dot pictures*.

Using scissors continues to present difficulties even when they are modified. The child will find it helpful if a border approximately 1cm wide is created around the picture. It is much easier to cut between lines than to try to manoeuvre scissors along the edge of the picture.

Perceptual skills

Parents and teachers will observe the perceptual problems experienced by the child in his drawings and collage. If the child is given the materials to reproduce a picture he will be unable to place the parts in the correct sequence on the page. In the example (Figure 6:2) the child was given 5 shaped pieces and asked to place them appropriately to represent the rocket. She could not fit the parts together to reproduce the whole.

Fig. 6:2 Amy, aged 5

The reception class teacher working with Amy has provided some suggestions for shape pictures and they are included in the appendices. A magnetic board* with a selection of shapes is an alternative method of developing the skill.

Encourage the child to build 3-dimensional models and play games guessing which pieces are farthest away.

The child may continue to find it difficult to cross his mid-line so activities should be developed to encourage him to do so. An example would be to ask the child to sit on the floor with his legs stretched out in front. Place 10 objects, 5 on either side of his thighs. Place a different coloured sticker or picture on the back of each hand to discriminate between left and right. The instructions would be: 'Pick up the ball with your right hand, the red sticker is on the back'.

Large piece jigsaw puzzles would be appropriate although at first the child may be reluctant to try them. There are also many computer programmes which develop the child's perceptual skills and concept of shape. Assess whether the child favours a mouse or joy-stick to control the movement of the arrow.

Developmental
— Dyspraxia

Always try to minimise the level of difficulty when there is a motor skill component involved in any activity.

Language development

By the age of 5 the dyspraxic child will have acquired the skills necessary to communicate verbally in sentences of 5+ syllables. He will continue to use gestures to convey meaning and this will involve him in higher levels of motor activity. The teacher should make allowances for this behaviour and not perceive it as the child being deliberately disruptive.

Information conveyed verbally takes longer to process and the dyspraxic child will rarely respond immediately to requests. Repeat instructions and remind all of the pupils what is required. The child must be included as part of the class group and not continually singled out for negative attention.

Listening skills should be extended and this could be a valuable exercise for all pupils. Ask the children to sit quietly with their eyes closed and arrange for a series of sounds to be made in different parts of the room. When the child has learned to focus on the direction of the sound he will be able to listen and respond more appropriately to the voice of the teacher.

Language development is dependent on the ability to sequence information and reproduce it verbally. Some of the commercial programmes designed to develop such skills are available from the Ayres Collection. The titles include 'Visual sequencing cards', 'Visual auditory sequencing on tape' and 'Sequential thinking cards'. In addition there is a series of picture cards and the child is asked 'What's wrong'. This generates discussion about the event but the activity must be completed with an adult.

Additional information

The child should be given personal targets to achieve in the areas of greatest concern. Reduce the distractions in the classroom and give constant reminders to encourage the child to remain on task. Offer the appropriate praise whether it is verbal, giving the child a sticker, or recording progress on a chart. Always find something positive to say during the session; children at this age work not for themselves but for the approval of the teacher or another adult.

Arrange activities so that the child is able to work with a small group within the class. Find some means of attaching the paper or book to the desk to stop it moving while the child is trying to draw or write. The classroom environment must be adapted to suit the child as he may find it impossible to adapt to it.

Activities for children in years 1 and 2

After leaving the reception class the learning environment is even more structured and child and teacher are under pressure to achieve specified levels in curricular attainments. There is less opportunity for the child to become involved in programmes to develop gross motor skills during the school day. By the age of 6 a child will usually have had the opportunity to experience a variety of activities which would extend his ability to co-ordinate motor movement. As stated earlier, the dyspraxic child cannot acquire these skills naturally. He must be offered a programme which breaks down the skills into smaller steps and teaches them in a sequential manner. The exercise programme detailed in chapter 7 is suitable for youngsters from the age of 6 who have motor learning difficulties. The entry point on the programme is dependent on the ability of the child, not his age, and is therefore suitable for any child or young adult with perceptual-motor problems.

Classroom environment

seating should allow the child to rest both feet flat on the floor

desk should be at elbow height with the facility to use a sloping surface for reading and additional activities

the child should be placed so he is able to view the teacher directly without turning his body

make prepared recording sheets available to reduce the quantity of handwriting required

use lined paper with spaces sufficiently wide to accommodate the child's handwriting

attach the paper to the desk to avoid the unnecessary distress of having to hold it in position with one hand while trying to draw or write with the other

reinforce verbal instructions by repeating them several times

allow extra time for the completion of a task.

Extension activities

Gross motor skills

Design either an individual programme or involve a small group of pupils selecting activities from the programme outlined in the next chapter. Completing a baseline assessment and the selection of targets is also discussed in chapter 7.

Developmental
— **Dyspraxia**

Fine motor skills

The child will be starting to master the reproduction of letter shapes. He will continue to have difficulty placing the letter or numeral in the correct position on the page. Prepared sheets with columns already drawn which require the child to write only the answer reduce the stress of setting out the work. Aids for ensuring the correct pencil grip may continue to be necessary. Physical pressure required to produce handwritten material can be exhausting for the dyspraxic child. Some youngsters also exhibit a mild tremor which becomes more noticeable when they become anxious. Computer-assisted learning can reduce pressure to produce written material but it should not be viewed as a substitute for handwriting.

Perceptual skills

Difficulties may persist with the child's awareness of connecting shapes. He can reproduce drawings of people and objects but they are misrepresented. Figure 6:3 is an illustration. Although Ian has included all the components of the house and the cat they are incorrectly positioned when he has re-assembled the parts into the whole. The house has 4 windows, a door, a roof and smoke coming from the chimney. Ian is able to produce the squares and rectangles appropriately. The cat presented more complex problems. Many of the shapes are irregular and while the face is centralised in the body, the ears and whiskers are external. The Frostig visual-perceptual programme* offers a variety of materials which develop these skills in young children.

When the dyspraxic child is required to understand new concepts he should have access to multi-sensory methods of instruction. The Multi-link* materials encourage the child to develop number skills using blocks and coloured templates. This scheme is extended to MathSafari* which offers challenging activities to explore aspects of mathematics including shape, space, position and rotational symmetry. Pupils learn at their own pace by manipulating pieces of Multi-link in order to problem-solve.

Language development

By the age of 6 or 7 the dyspraxic child may have compensated for his early delayed language skills. He may have an extensive vocabulary but not learned the social rules of conversation. He does not wait for the person speaking to finish, he makes his ideas known as they occur to him. In addition his voice may be loud with poor tone. The teacher needs to be aware of the potential difficulties which may arise if other members of the class pass adverse comments every time he speaks. More time will have to be spent encouraging the child to respond appropriately in class either when asked a direct question or taking his turn as part of the larger group. Allowances should be made for his uncontrollable enthusiasm but firm clear instructions should reinforce the expected behaviour.

Fig. 6:3 *Drawings by Ian, aged 6*

A house

A cat

── **Dyspraxia**

Many dyspraxic children are able to read well but if asked to read aloud their presentation is hesitant. Spelling may present some problems but having to record information in writing is their greatest cause of anxiety. Their speed of processing information is reduced and sequencing tasks such as story-writing may prove to be extremely difficult. It would help the child if he could be given sentences or paragraphs to sequence instead of having to write the entire story on paper. Give the child the opportunity to record his work on tape and give oral presentations.

Additional information

The dyspraxic child can appear to be excitable and highly-emotional. This is usually linked to the frustration experienced when he is unable to complete tasks to his satisfaction. It is important for the child to have personal targets set for him so he does not see himself in competition with the rest of his peer group. Set targets which are achievable in the short term, perhaps over a period of 1 or 2 weeks so he can observe his progress. Always find something to praise every day to break the cycle of failure he may already have experienced.

Simplify tasks and reduce the added anxiety to a minimum. On days when PE is part of the timetable let the child wear clothing which can be removed easily.

Always allow extra time for the child to finish the task or reduce the quantity required. A child who is told he has to stay behind in class to complete unfinished work soon becomes disaffected, especially when he is trying as hard as he is able.

Chapter

7

Remediation programmes for the older pupil

$\mathcal{T}$he most effective interventions I have undertaken with children aged 6 and over have involved access to structured exercise programmes. The purpose of this chapter is to explain each activity in detail and identify targets which would indicate the child's mastery of that particular skill. It may be several weeks before the child is able to achieve the specified target but he would be set individual targets in the preceding weeks. For example: if the child is able to balance independently on his right foot for 2 seconds the final target could be to achieve 10+ seconds. The first week's target might be 4 seconds, extending it as he develops his skills. When the recommended target is achieved the child should move to the next activity.

Activities should be selected from the programme which build on emerging skills. Do not choose an activity in which the child at the outset is unable to achieve any degree of success. Select one from earlier in the programme where the child is halfway to meeting the target. Between 15 and 20 minutes should be spent each day working on the exercise programme. Younger pupils usually follow up to a maximum of 8 activities while older junior age and secondary pupils are able to complete between 10 and 15.

The activities are organised into different sections:

- finger, hand and arm movements

- hand-eye co-ordination

- foot-eye co-ordination

- balance

- whole body co-ordination

- sound and movement.

Assessment of the child will highlight strengths and weaknesses. Select some activities in which he may develop skills quickly and some which are more difficult. Provide the child with an individual programme and encourage him to record his own progress.

Developmental —— Dyspraxia

Section 1: Finger, hand and arm movements

	Activity	Target
1	The child may have difficulty using each finger independently. Moving the index finger may result in the others having to extend simultaneously. Use finger puppets, either the type which fit over the finger or draw faces directly on to the fleshy tip. Initially encourage the child to use only the index finger of one hand and extend the programme until the fingers of each hand are able to move independently. Farmyard animals and nursery rhyme characters make the exercise more enjoyable. **Observe** Associated mirror movement with uninvolved fingers on the same and opposite hand. It will help the child master the skill if initially he is able to rest all of his fingers, except the one required to move, on the edge of the table.	To move each finger independently of any other.
2	Use 2 finger puppets (index and second finger) to co-ordinate 2 fingers in opposition to the rest of the hand. **Observe** Whether the right hand fingers move without associated movements in the left and vice versa. If associated movements are in evidence encourage the child to hold a small ball in his uninvolved hand or place it flat on the table surface.	To move two fingers simultaneously on each hand in a co-ordinated manner without associated movements in the other.
3	Use whole-hand puppet to co-ordinate 3 fingers appropriately. **Observe** This skill will be mastered easily if activities 1 and 2 have been taught previously.	To manipulate a hand puppet appropriately.
4	The child should first place his right hand and then his left on 5 sequential white notes on a keyboard. The notes should be numbered 1-5. **Comments** Develop the child's ability to play the notes forward with confidence before attempting them in reverse.	To play the notes in sequence 1-5. Then in reverse with each hand in 5 seconds.

5	The child should place each hand separately on the keyboard as before on notes numbered 1-5. **Comments** Say the numbers slowly to give the child time to process the information.	An adult will direct the child. Play separate notes not in sequence e.g.3-5-2-1-4 without hesitation. Child to achieve 5/5 success.
6	Two chime bars placed in front of the child 5 cm apart. Child to use striker in each hand alternately. First right hand then the left. **Comments** Improves flexibility in up and down and sideways movement in the wrist. Eliminate associated movements and tongue-thrust if evident.	Chime bars 20 cm apart. Child to strike each in turn 10/10 times in 10 seconds.
7	Give the child a small marble and ask him to manipulate it slowly between the thumb and index finger of each hand. **Comments** The child requires visual feedback so try to extend the activity when he child has mastered the skill to manoeuvre the marble with his eyes closed.	To manipulate the marble for 30 seconds with the thumb and index finger of each hand.
8	Ask the child to repeat the activity described in 7, manipulating the marble between the thumb and successive fingers on each hand. **Comments** Tongue-thrusts are common so encourage the child to keep his teeth and lips together.	To manipulate the marble for 20 seconds between the thumb and successive fingers on each hand.
9	Tie a skipping rope 3 m in length to a secure support. Ask the child to hold the other end initially in his right hand and then in the left. The child should be positioned so that the rope, when held, is a few centimetres from the floor. The child is asked to turn the rope in a wide arc from the shoulder. **Comments** Initially there will be problems when the child tries to achieve regular movement. It is important that the skill is mastered in the first instance with the arm extended.	

10	Repeat the activity outlined above with the right and left hands holding the rope. Hold elbows to the waist and turn the rope from the elbow. **Comments** The child may use his whole arm to start the rope turning, bring elbows in to the waist quickly.	Turn the rope x 30 with each hand.
11	Repeat the activity, turning the rope from the wrist. Hold elbows to the waist for additional stability. **Comments** In activities 9, 10 and 11 observe associated movements such as tongue-thrusts, motions in the opposing arm and whether the child is able to keep his feet still while turning the rope. It is important that these additional movements are eliminated.	Turn the rope x 30 with each hand.

Section 2: Hand-eye co-ordination

	Activity	Target
1	Ask the child to hold a bean bag in each hand. Begin with both hands touching below the waist. Slowly lift hands along the mid-line of the body until both arms are extended above the head. Separate the hands and bring slowly down towards each side of the body until hands touch again below the waist. See diagram. **Comments** The child may have difficulty executing the action in a fluid manner. He may also move one arm more quickly than the other. Ensure that the actions in both arms are at the same speed. 	Repeat movement, co-ordinating both hands simultaneously x 10.
2	Blow a number of large bubbles into an open space. Ask the child to 'pop' them by clapping hands together on each bubble. **Comment** Use the correct fluid as children become very impatient when the bubbles burst before leaving the dispenser. Blow the bubbles within reach of the child to reduce the requirement to chase after them.	To burst as many bubbles as possible in 2 minutes.
3	Repeat activity 2, allowing the child to burst the bubbles with a large-surface bat. Use each hand for half the allocated time. **Comments** This task extends the child's ability to co-ordinate his hands and arms.	To burst as many bubbles as possible, 1 minute for each hand.

4	Place the child in a low kneeling position 3 metres away from the target. The most popular target is a set of 6 skittles placed 10 cm apart in front of the child. Ask the child to roll a tennis ball or equivalent to knock over the skittles. Use the right hand initially and then the left. **Comments** Gradually extend the child's distance from the target until he is able to achieve the same degree of success at 5 metres distance.	5/6 skittles in 2 attempts right hand. 5/6 skittles in 2 attempts, left hand. 5/6 skittles in 2 attempts, first with right then left hand.
5	Standing feet together, give the child 5 bean bags. Place in basket (waste paper size) 3 metres away. Instruct the child to throw the bean bags one at a time into the basket. Throw 5x underarm with the right hand then 5x underarm with the left. Repeat both with overarm throw. **Comments** Use the bean bags to reduce the amount of time the youngsters spend chasing after balls which have missed the target.	4/5 success with right and left hands using underarm and overarm throw.
6	The extension activity for older pupils would require placing the target 5 metres from the child. Increase the number of attempts with each hand to 10. **Comments** As the child becomes more competent, encourage him to stand with the opposing feet in front while throwing. For example, if he is throwing with his right arm, his left foot should be placed forward to counter-balance his movement. Again observe any associated movements.	8/10 successes with right and left hands using underarm and overarm throw.
7	Line 5 targets (skittles, plastic bottles, boxes) in a row at 4 metres distance and shoulder height. Give the child 5 bean bags or small soft balls and ask him to throw with his preferred hand. **Comments** A child of 9+ years will need to establish dominance and improve the skills in his preferred hand. Ensure that the opposing foot is placed in front of the body when child takes aim.	4/5 success in 2 attempts.

8	With two hands encourage the child to hold a large sponge ball at waist height, bounce it once, then catch it using both hands. **Comments** The child must look at the ball because he will have difficulty judging the speed of the ball returning from the bounce.	Bounce and catch x 10 in succession.
9	When the child has mastered activity 8 allow him to throw the ball, with a single bounce to another pupil or adult. The ball should be returned in the same way. The pupils should be positioned 3 metres apart. **Comments** The child may become very excited waiting for the ball to be returned. Encourage him to stand still by providing a small ring or square in which to stand.	10 complete catches in 40 seconds.
10	Bounce a large ball repeatedly on the floor, first with the right hand then the left. **Comments** The unused hand may be held in a clenched position. Give the child a small ball or baton to hold to extend the fingers. Observe and remove associated movements.	10 consecutive bounces with each hand.
11	Place a target 20 cm in diameter initially 2 then extending to 4 metres distance from the pupil. Throw a large sponge ball placed at chin height towards the target. Use both hands together. **Comments** Place the target at the distance when the child can initially achieve success 4/10 times. When this is raised to 9/10 move the target farther away to a maximum of 4 metres.	9/10 success.
12	For the older pupil, 10 + years, use a wall mounted or free standing basketball ring. The youngster should stand 2 metres away and throw x 10 with hands together and x 10 with hands separately. **Comments** If the child is unable to achieve 2 or more scores in his first attempt spend more time on activity 11.	To throw the ball through the ring with success of 6 or more in 10 attempts.

13	At this stage in the programme the child should be able to judge more accurately the speed and direction of the throw. Develop throwing and catching skills without bouncing the ball. Position pupil and adult/peer 3 metres apart. They should throw a large sponge ball between one another x 10. **Comments** Ensure that both participants are at a level of ability where success will be achieved on 4/10 throws otherwise frustration will be evident.	10/10 is the final target for this activity.
14	Extend activity 13 using a small sponge ball. The thrower should use right hand x 10 and then the left hand x 10. The ball should be caught in both hands. **Comments** Do not embark on this activity until skills 1-13 in this section have been mastered	4/5 balls caught when thrown with the right hand. 4/5 balls caught when thrown with the left hand.
15	Place 2 obstacles (cones) 1 metre apart. The child should initially stand 2 metres away. Place a small sponge ball at the feet of the child and instruct him to direct it between the posts using a bat or hockey stick. **Comments** The child should hold the stick with both hands, standing sideways to the target. If he is right-side dominant, his left side should be facing the target; The converse if he is left-sided.	8/10.
16	Extend activity 15 until the child is able to achieve the same level of success 4 metres from the target. **Comments** Wait until he has achieved success of 8/10 at 2 metres before moving the target farther away.	8/10.

Section 3: Foot-eye co-ordination

	Activity	Target
1	Mark two parallel lines on the floor, 6 metres long and 20 cm apart. Ask the child to walk heel-to-toe forwards and backwards between the lines. **Comments** Shorten the distance to 3 metres forwards and backwards if the child has difficulty completing the task. Examine the position of the hands and arms. The fist may be clenched. If so give the child an object, eg. tennis ball or baton to hold. Heavier objects provide the child with increased stability. Extend the distance and remove the hand- held objects when appropriate until the child achieves the target with hands and arms held in a relaxed manner on either side of the body.	To walk forwards and backwards without stepping outside the parallel lines.
2	Using the parallel lines from activity 1, ask the child to walk on tiptoes forwards and backwards along the distance of 6 metres. **Comments** On tiptoes the child is more likely to move with hands clenched. As described in activity 1 give the child an object to hold in both hands to extend and reduce the tension in the fingers.	To walk forwards and backwards without stepping outside the parallel lines.
3	Again using the parallel lines, ask the child to walk on his heels forwards and backwards. This activity requires greater physical effort than walking on toes so the measured distance should be reduced to 4 metres. **Comments** The child may walk with hands extended upwards. It is important that the hands are brought down and this can be achieved either by placing them in pockets or holding slightly heavier objects than those described in activities 1 and 2. When the child is able to hold his hands in a relaxed position, remove weights.	To walk forwards and backwards a distance of 4 metres without stepping outside the parallel lines.

4	Use the parallel lines and instruct the child to walk sideways along the 6 metre distance, leading with his right foot one way and his left foot the other. **Comments** Observe any associated movements and ensure that they are reduced.	To travel the distance up an down in 20 seconds.
5	Use the parallel lines and place 4 obstacles across. Mini-hurdles* are ideal otherwise arrange for obstacles to be 30 cm high. The child is instructed to walk between the lines and 'climb' over the obstacles. **Comments** Initially it may be necessary to place obstacles only 5 cm high so the child achieves success.	To walk the distance up and down in 18 seconds without knocking over the obstacles or standing outside the parallel lines.
6	If the 'stepping stones' apparatus is available as described in the previous chapter the child should walk along on his toes, one foot on each step. **Comments** Observe the hand position and extend fingers if clenched.	To move along the beam without stepping off.
7	Place two posts/cones 1 metre apart. Place a large sponge ball 3 metres away. From a standing position shoot at the gap, first with the right foot then the left. **Comments** Observe position of arms and hands. Minimise associated movements.	4/5 successes with the right then the left foot.
8	Extension of activity 7. Increase the distance to 6 metres and shoot at the target, right foot then left. **Comments** Gradually extend the distance from 3 to 6 metres. Establish a baseline where the child consistently can achieve a score of 2/5. It may be necessary to vary the distance for each foot.	4/5 successes with the right then the left foot.

9	Mark out squares for the game of 'hopscotch' with 5 'hops' and 5 'jumps'. The child begins on the single square, standing on one foot and moves on jumping with both feet. **Comments** Demonstrate the activity and start by using half the grid. If the child has problems with balance give him a large sponge ball to hold with both hands. Keeping the arms and hands into the body improves the child's stability. As he masters the skill, remove the ball.	To move along the grid appropriately.
10	If there is access to a large surface area and a scooter can be obtained, foot-eye co-ordination may be further extended. This is a very difficult skill to master and the child should concentrate on placing his leading foot on the platform and propelling the scooter with the other leg. **Comments** This activity should be developed at home rather than in school.	To propel the scooter around the circuit.
11	Stampabouts* look like two upturned plastic beakers which are threaded at the top. The strings are kept taut and the child balances one foot on each cup. They are based on the same principle as stilts but require a little less foot-eye co-ordination. A distance of 4 metres would seem appropriate. **Comments** Aids which provide added interest to the co-ordination activities in this section are not essential but add fun.	To be able to walk on the cups a distance of 4 metres.

Section 4: Balance

	Activity	Target
1	Ask the child to balance on each foot separately. Initially allow him to hold the back of a chair or touch the wall lightly. As the child becomes more competent encourage him to stand without support. Then demonstrate the activity, balancing on one foot and holding a bean bag in each hand with arms outstretched on either side. Ask the child to copy. **Comments** Develop the child's stability before asking him to stand unaided. The bean bags reduce the clenched movement in the fist and outstretched arms help improve balance.	To balance unaided for 10 seconds on each foot.
2	Extend activity 1 by asking the child to balance on separate feet standing on a variety of surfaces, e.g. sand, foam cushion, skipping rope. **Comments** Ensure that activity 1 is mastered before attempting different surfaces. Correct tongue-thrust if evident.	To balance unaided and on a variety of surfaces for 10 seconds on each foot.
3	A selection of wobble boards, as described in the previous chapter, develops a child's awareness of the centre of gravity in his body. Encourage the child to adjust his weight so it passes initially through one leg and then the other. **Comments.** Some boards have adjustable heights and offer an extension of this activity.	To manoeuvre the board for 20 seconds without falling off.
4	The child should develop the skills to enable him to walk along the length of a beam 10 cm wide, taking short steps. **Comments** Encourage the child to extend his arms and hold a tennis ball in each hand if the fist is clenched.	To walk slowly along the beam, arms outstretched without falling. Beam should be approximately 2 metres long.

5	Extend activity 4 by requiring the child to step over 2 small obstacles placed across the beam. **Comments** During the first few attempts hold the child's hand while he steps over the obstacles.	To walk the length of the beam in small steps.
6	Reduce the width of the beam to 5 cm, the base of an upturned bench is suitable, and repeat activities 4 and 5. **Comments** Wait until the child is confident balancing on the narrow beam before placing obstacles.	To walk the length of the narrowed beam in small steps without falling.
7	Give the child a short handled bat with a large surface area. Hold the bat horizontal and balance a bean bag on the top. Ask the child to walk 4 metres balancing the bean bag on the bat. Change hands and walk back over the distance. **Comments** Observe the unused hand. If it is clenched use a tennis ball to extend the fingers. If the unused arm is waving give the child a more substantial weight to carry, such as a baton.	Walk a distance of 4 metres, balancing the bean bag on the bat. Use the right hand first then the left.
8	Extend the activity to balancing a small sponge ball on the surface of the bat. Begin with a walking distance of 2 metres and extend it to 4 as the child masters the skill. **Comments** Check again for any associated movements and eliminate them.	Walk a distance of 4 metres with the ball balancing on the bat. Use the right hand then the left.
9	Ask the child to lie face downwards, resting his stomach on a skateboard. Legs should extend together in a straight line beyond the board. Using both hands together the child propels himself the distance of 4 metres. **Comments** The child must apply equal pressure with both hands or the board will deviate from a straight line.	Establish a baseline by timing the activity. Reduce the time by half.

10	Ask the child to sit on the skateboard with legs stretching out in front. Again using both hands simultaneously propel the board forwards along the 4 metre distance. **Comments** The child should lean forwards slightly to ensure that the centre of gravity is in front of the body.	Time the activity and reduce by half.
11	Ask the child to kneel on the skateboard and rest on his heels. Propel the board forwards using both hands along the 4 metre distance. **Comments** The child should again lean forward slightly to move the centre of gravity to the front of the body.	Reduce baseline time by half.
12	An extension activity is to develop the child's ability to co-ordinate movement on a small trampoline. The exercise is fun but is not a specific requirement of this programme. **Comments** The child should have the skills necessary to jump from a standing position on the floor before attempting this activity. Observe the child's hands and arms while jumping. If any tension is evident give him a large sponge ball to hold which can be removed as his skills develop.	To achieve 10+ continuous jumps without breaking the pattern of movement.
13	Using a Pedal-go* is another activity which provides enjoyment and improves balance; 2 platforms are positioned between 2 sets of wheels. The child propels himself forwards by placing his weight through one leg then the other. **Comments** A popular exercise for pupils of all ages. Keep arms down if they exhibit associated movements.	To move forwards a distance of 4+ metres.

Section 5: Whole body co-ordination

	Activity	Target
1	Provide the child with a box tunnel*. The child should crawl on hands and knees along the length of the apparatus. Check that he is able to co-ordinate hands and feet. Demonstrate the required movements. **Comments** Many dyspraxic youngsters never go through the crawling stage and find this activity very difficult. Continue until the child can co-ordinate movements reflexively.	To co-ordinate arms and legs to travel a distance of 4 metres.
2	Place a selection of cut-out hand and foot shapes along a 4 metre line. The child is asked to travel the distance on hands and feet. He may place his hand only over the corresponding shape, the same with his feet. **Comments** Establish a baseline by timing the child's movement from the start to the end of the line. Encourage him to achieve a faster time on subsequent days.	To travel the 4 metre distance using shapes appropriately.
3	Design an obstacle course comprising large bean bags, benches and an assortment of mats. The child is requested to crawl around on hands and knees. Establish a baseline by timing the child's first attempt at completing the course. Encourage him to achieve a faster time each day. **Comments** Ensure that the child is wearing suitable clothing. Smooth surfaced track suit bottoms are the most comfortable.	To achieve a faster time each day. Discontinue after 10 days.
4	Ask the child to walk at medium pace around the sides of the gymnasium or playground. Observe the whole body movement. Note the position of the hands and whether the child extends his right arm when placing his left foot forward. **Comments** Co-ordination of arms and legs may not occur naturally and the skills will need to be broken down into their components and taught.	Establish flexible co-ordinated body movement while walking

Developmental
— Dyspraxia

The classroom environment can be adapted to meet the needs of the dyspraxic child and minimise the anxiety frequently experienced. Figure 7:2 is an example of a 9-year-old pupil's handwritten story.

Daniel is a very articulate youngster who is an avid reader of nature books. Everything about animals and their habits is of great interest to him. During his science lessons he constantly questions how and why things work. His task was to produce an imaginative story. This was something he could really enjoy. He chose as his subject a skeleton. He explored the plight of the little skeleton who wants to 'learn things'. He is unable to attend school so night classes are suggested. Daniel spent the entire session completing his handwritten script. He had included a drawing to add interest.

The work, when presented to his class teacher, appeared untidy and was almost impossible to read. This was Daniel's best effort. He had produced a wonderful story which could have been easily disregarded had the class teacher not been aware of his difficulty.

Daniel was invited to read his story aloud and it was processed on the computer by the teacher. Daniel's exercise book still contains his handwritten story with the translation on the facing page.

How different the picture might have been. As is the case for so many dyspraxic pupils, handwritten work is judged on form rather than content. Asking the child to rewrite the story does not bring any visible improvements; it merely adds to the child's frustration and further lowers his self-esteem.

Fig. 7:2 *The story of little skeleton by Daniel, aged 9*

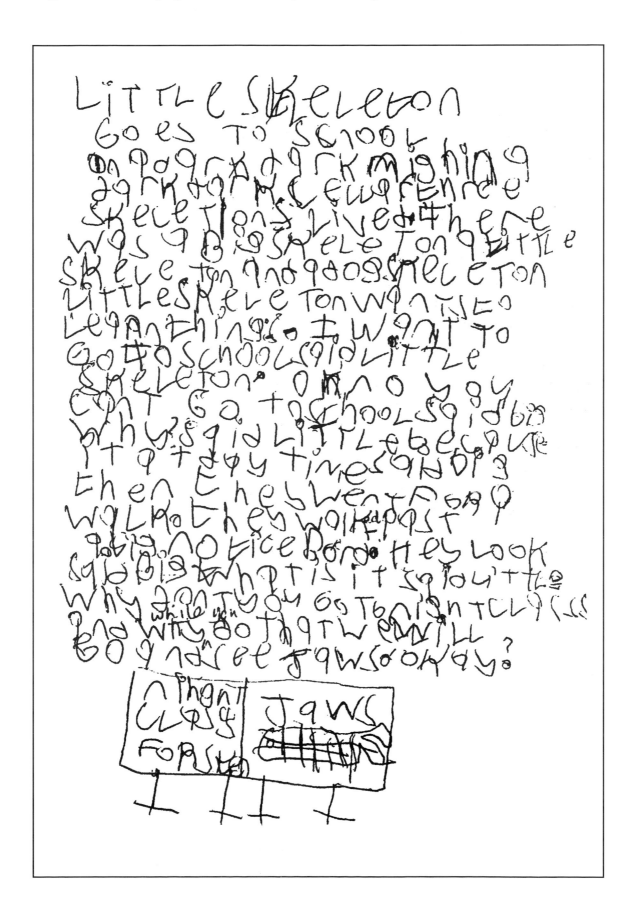

Developmental
— Dyspraxia

An explanation as to why the handwriting of dyspraxic youngsters follows this characteristic pattern was offered by Ellis in 1987. He describes handwriting as a complex perceptual-motor skill which requires visual and kinaesthetic feedback, at least part of the time, to execute the correct movements. A controlled experiment was carried out in which a group of unaffected subjects were placed in circumstances which prevented them monitoring and controlling their handwriting. Visual feedback (sight of the hand and the pen) was eliminated by obscuring the sight of the writing hand and an additional task, either counting or tapping, was included to interfere with the writers' ability to attend to kinaesthetic feedback. Research showed that unlike the unaffected subjects, the dyspraxic pupils' writing was no more error-prone with eyes closed than when they were open. It appears therefore that dyspraxic pupils are permanently unable to use visual feedback to monitor for errors or help correct them. In addition, when the dyspraxic child has his forefinger moved, with eyes closed, to form a letter shape, he experiences great difficulty using kinaesthetic information to identify letters.

Figure 7:3 shows the handwriting samples of two 10-year-old pupils. Example A was 'free' writing while B was completed with eyes closed. Pupil 1 was dyspraxic pupil 2 the control.

Fig. 7:3 Pupil 1 handwriting samples

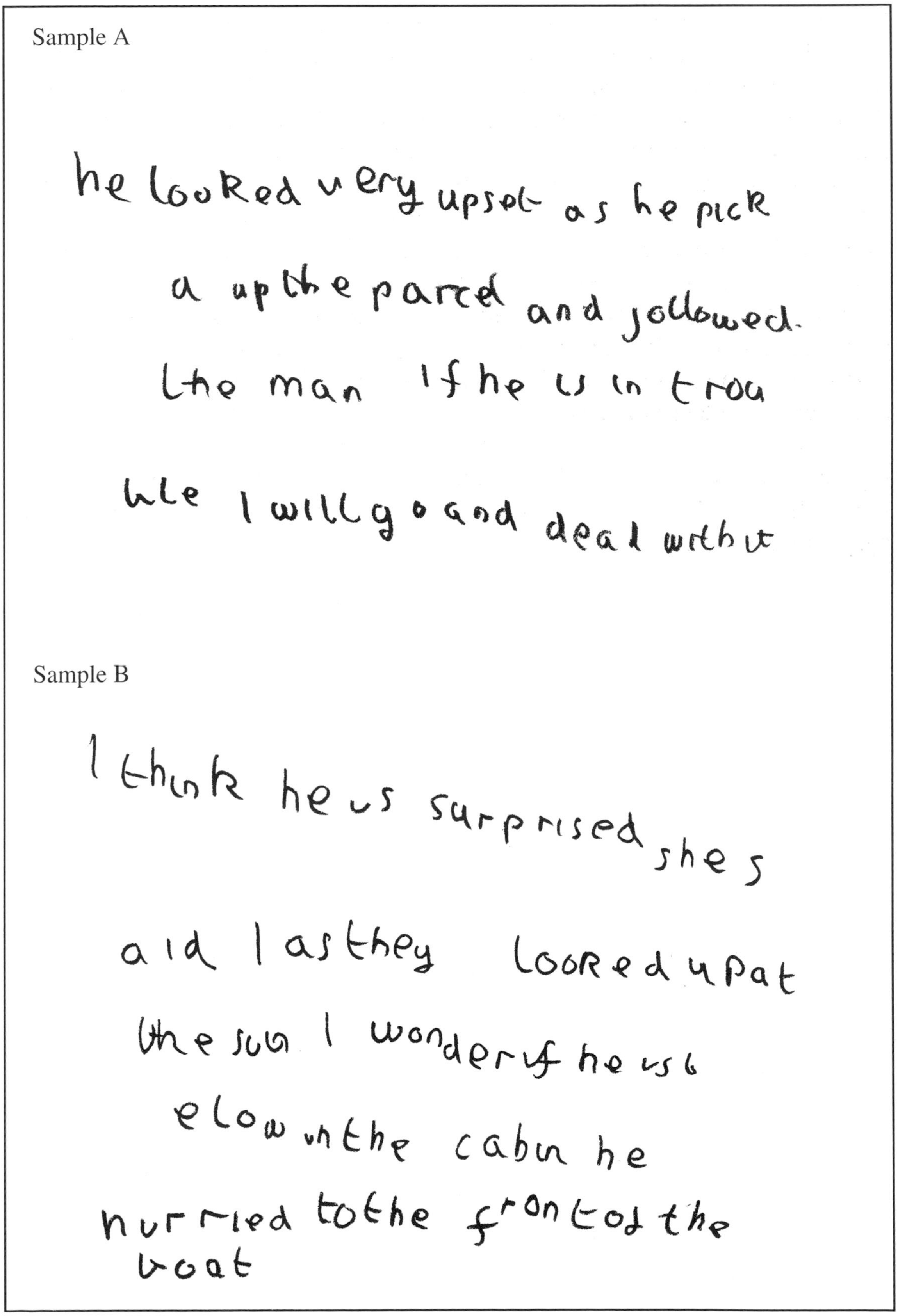

Sample A

he looked very upset as he pick
a up the parcel and jollowed.
the man if he us in troa
ble I will g o and deal with it

Sample B

I think he us surprised she s
aid I as they looked u Pat
the sun I wonder if he us l
e low in the cabin he
hurried to the front of the
boat

Pupil 2 handwriting samples

Sample A

Soon the rest of the household was awake. The noise was very loud and came from the garden .

Sample B

As he was trying to make up his mind to call out for help his foot met nothing but air

Writing patterns exhibited by the majority of dyspraxic youngsters are termed dysgraphic. Writing begins as a linguistic process and ends as one which is perceptual-motor. It is unsurprising, therefore, that dyspraxic youngsters, many of whom have problems developing early language skills and who subsequently exhibit perceptual-motor difficulties, find handwriting an almost impossible skill to master.

By the age of 8 or 9 the child will be well aware of tasks he finds difficult and will have developed an extensive repertoire of avoidance tactics. They will range from forgetting books, writing materials and the PE kit to the appearance of physical symptoms such as headaches and sickness on particular mornings. In addition, the child's unco-ordinated movements are dismissed as careless behaviour. If left untreated a pattern will emerge of:

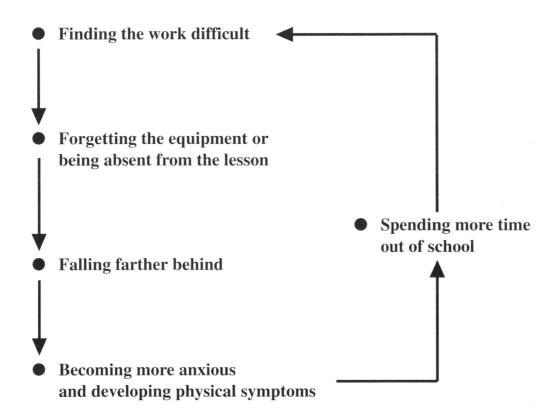

- **Finding the work difficult**

- **Forgetting the equipment or being absent from the lesson**

- **Falling farther behind**

- **Spending more time out of school**

- **Becoming more anxious and developing physical symptoms**

It is the responsibility of the class teacher to provide differentiated programmes of work to meet the needs of the individuals. No child wants to fail so it is important that he feels capable of achieving something which is valued by his teacher. Pupils of primary age are not usually self-motivated to work hard; they do so to obtain praise from their parents and teachers.

Fig. 7:4

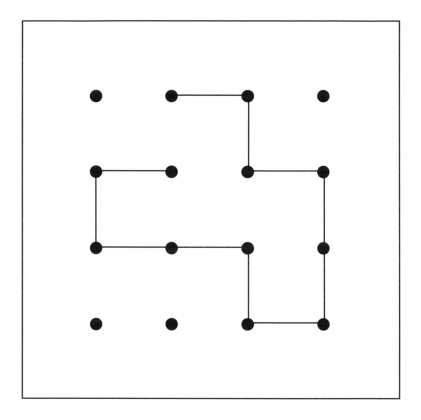

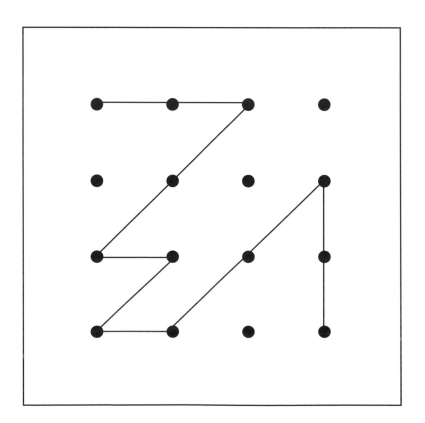

Perceptual skills

Access to the Frostig programme will offer extension activities for the 9 to 11-year-old pupils. In addition the child will acquire perceptual skills more easily if he has a good understanding of two-dimensional shapes. Clear templates are provided in Appendix 1, of the patterns which aid development.

See Figure 7:4. Present the child with the sheet comprising two large squares of 16 dots joined by horizontal and vertical lines. The child then copies the shapes which should become more complex as his skills develop.

When the child is competent in completing the large shapes provide him with the prepared template of 12 smaller dot shapes and his own unused recording sheet. Provide the template for 5 consecutive days. The child is timed and encouraged to improve on the time of the previous day. Ensure that the template is presented with the same starting figure on the top left corner. When the child is able to copy the shapes in 60 seconds, rotate the template and start the programme again. When the skills are mastered the activity can be extended by presenting the child with patterns which follow a diagonal line. The transition to this activity may present some problems initially, so begin with only 3 boxes instead of 12.

Language development

This becomes less of a problem as the child gets older. If reading aloud to the class group is required check whether the child feels sufficiently confident to do so. The sequencing of ideas in story-writing may cause some concerns so discuss with the child how the events develop and provide a story planner for him. This might be achieved best by producing a series of 3 line drawings depicting the beginning middle and the end. This idea may benefit many other pupils in the class.

Additional information

If the child has not been able to access some parts of the curriculum during earlier school years because of his limited perceptual skills, he should be given the opportunity to rediscover basic concepts in subject areas like mathematics. N.E.S. Arnold has produced a range of materials designed for such pupils in the top end of primary and the lower end of secondary education. The concepts are delivered through practical activities and use the multi-link blocks. The basics are taught through the number skills plus programme and handbooks are provided which relate specifically to levels 1-3 of the National Curriculum.

Extension programmes are:

- rediscovering fractions
- shape and space
- towards algebra through structures.

In all areas of the curriculum set targets where the child is judged against his own efforts and not by comparison with the rest of the class. Raise the child's position in the group by giving him a post of responsibility, whether that is to collect finished work from all pupils or to be allowed to tidy the chairs at lunchtime. The responsible task may enable the teacher to involve the child working with another pupil if he has relationship difficulties with class members.

Try to predict situations which may cause anxiety and offer alternatives. If teams are to be selected, the teacher should divide the class. It is always a humiliating experience to be the one left at the end. If the system in operation at lunchtime requires children to carry trays of food to their tables, arrange the seating so the dyspraxic child has the shortest distance to travel. Reduce the number of opportunities to single out the dyspraxic pupils for negative attention, either by staff or peers.

School environment for pupils of secondary age

Transfer to secondary education can present anxieties for many pupils but perhaps more so for the dyspraxic child. As highlighted in previous chapters, visual perceptual tasks require a greater processing time. Finding the correct room and following a timetable to attend the specific lesson is a skill which takes longer to acquire. At the outset the child needs to develop a close relationship with a personal tutor who is aware of his needs. Getting lost is an excuse for many youngsters to avoid the lesson; this may not be the case for the dyspraxic child. In secondary school where there are many different subject teachers it may not be possible for them to have the same awareness of the child's problem as the personal tutor. There is increasing likelihood that a supply teacher who has no knowledge of the child will be covering the class. It is for these reasons that the child has to be able to confide in a concerned member of staff who can present his case to the teacher who is annoyed that X is late for the lesson and has produced only half of the expected amount of written work.

The difficulties are greatly alleviated if the pupil has gained peer acceptance. Too often he finds he is in conflict not only with the teacher but also the rest of the class. Peer group acceptance emerged as the most significant factor in my research with secondary age pupils in determining the child's motivation and attitude towards school.

The child should be placed in groups according to his intellectual ability which at first may be difficult to judge if indecipherable written work is used as a criterion. If the child is placed inappropriately he will not be motivated by the lesson-content, and behavioural difficulties will emerge.

Try to involve the pupil in organised lunchtime activities. Dyspraxic children who are not accepted by their peers can easily become the victims of bullying. Many pupils gain great benefits from a homework club.

- they are able to discuss classwork which has caused concern

- they are with other pupils who require additional adult help and they view themselves less as being the only child with difficulties

- it is easier to establish relationships within a small group.

Subject teachers covering topics which require good spatial awareness, for example map reading and technical drawing, should be made aware of the additional support requirement for a pupil with motor learning difficulties. In other subjects where dictated material is presented to the group the dyspraxic child should be allowed to record the information on tape as he is unable to listen and write at the same time.

The exercise programme proved most effective with pupils of secondary age. Most encouraging results were achieved when dyspraxic pupils were paired with other youngsters from within the school who were responsible for completing the record sheet. Their profile in the school was raised and peer group acceptance achieved. Close liaison between parents and school is essential to ensure that any difficulties are addressed quickly before unnecessary distress is caused to the pupil.

Dyspraxic students, post-16

Provision for students in colleges of further education is available if they are identified as having special educational needs. Increased access to computer-assisted learning reduces the quantity of work recorded manually. The environment can be adapted more easily for older pupils who can identify for themselves the parts of the curriculum causing particular difficulties.

It is helpful if students can make taped recordings in some lessons which alleviates concerns that important aspects of the course are missed. The student should be offered open access to a word-processor so that he is able to produce assignments which are legible and reflect his ability in the subject. Tutors should ensure that additional time is allocated to dyspraxic students for the production of their work and special consideration should be given for examinations.

Dyspraxic youngsters usually adapt well to the less structured environment in college when non-contact time is allocated to all students for research into their subjects and work preparation. The areas which had previously presented so many difficulties are, by choice, no longer part of the curriculum. Although access to motor skill programmes will alleviate some of their presenting problems, students should concentrate on working towards their strengths. Some of those interviewed had already discussed the possibility of obtaining qualifications to enable them to work with 'special needs' children and adults.

They said that personal experience had given them some understanding of the anxieties suffered when learning difficulties are not diagnosed and appropriate support is not available.

Social environment

At the age of 17 pressure mounts with the increasing expectation that a driving test will be passed. It is difficult enough trying to co-ordinate the movements to ride a bicycle: mastering the skills of driving a car presents even greater problems.

Limited peripheral vision is common among dyspraxic students and they can be unaware of what is happening around them. Driving does not just involve co-ordinating arm and leg movements but requires acute awareness of the car's position in space and speed of travelling. In addition the behaviour of other motorists must be considered.

In the sample, 5 students had some experience of driving. Of those 2 were having driving lessons although 1 had settled for an automatic.

The answer is to break down the skills into smaller steps like the activity programme described in chapter 7. Practise the skill for short periods each day instead of spending several hours every weekend. The student will need to build confidence in himself and his instructor.

Although research into dyspraxia is predominantly directed towards younger pupils there is evidence that access to specified developmental motor skill programmes improves concentration, co-ordination and perceptual ability regardless of age.

Chapter
8

Epilogue

*P*revious chapters have examined recent research into dyspraxia and considered ways of identifying from an early age children who have the condition. Motor learning difficulties, the research tells us, are evident in a large proportion of youngsters who have failed in the educational system and find themselves placed in residential institutions for those experiencing emotional and behavioural difficulties or clinical depression. If preventative measures can be introduced which provide remediation programmes for those youngsters the population currently requiring alternative and often very expensive provision will be reduced.

All disciplines in health, education and social services must work co-operatively with parents to ensure that these children are correctly diagnosed. Too frequently their difficulties are dismissed as being the result of:

- behavioural problems
- poor diet
- bad parenting
- frequent changes of school
- attention-seeking.

A detailed assessment of the child and subsequent access to specified remediation programmes can bring about dramatic social, emotional and educational improvements.

Resources available for children with special educational needs are finite whether that means access to professional time or specialised equipment. If we say constantly that there is not time and insufficient expertise to provide treatment then we are undervaluing ourselves and the commitment of parents.

Programmes which have been successful are described in detail. The sources of materials are listed in the appendices and some identified outside agencies which can offer support have been provided. The contents of the appendices are free from copyright and may be reproduced.

In addition to the remediation programmes, the environment in school and at home must be examined. The following factors are important:

- remove stress from the child
- always find something positive to acknowledge
- set personal attainable targets

- allow sufficient time for the completion of work

- integrate the child within his peer group

- even though the child exhibits poor attentional skills he will have good understanding. Always match the curriculum to ability

- give the child time every day to discuss his anxieties

- decide which behaviours are evident because of the condition and which are not: do not use dyspraxia as an excuse.

Regardless of the child's age, he should be encouraged to develop his gross and fine motor skills. Generally society is less physically active than 50 years ago. Many children spend a large part of their time watching television, videos and 'glued' to the computer screen. Could this explain why increasing numbers of children are being identified? Another question still unanswered is:

> *Are there more children now who exhibit motor learning difficulties, or are we becoming more skilled at making a diagnosis?*

Whatever the correct answer, dyspraxic children have represented a significant educational underclass, largely misjudged, frequently maligned and extensively ignored. They are indeed children with 'special needs'.

We now have a greater understanding of their difficulties and are more able to meet their needs. We must work towards restoring their self-esteem.

Appendix A - 1

Activity	Mon	Tues	Wed	Thur	Fri	Sat	Sun	Target

Name...................Class.................Activity Co-ordinator.................Date.................

Comments:-

Appendix A - 2

Motor Skills Screening		
Name..**Date**..........................**Age**.................		
Activity	Behaviour	Date
1. Walking on toes forwards and backwards		
2. Walking on heels forwards and backwards		
3. Walking on insides of feet		
4. Walking on outsides of feet		
5. Recognising fingers touched when obscured from view. Right hand then left		

6. Finger sequencing - right then left		
7. Wrist rotation		
8. Balancing on each foot		
9. Touching end of nose with index finger of each hand (eyes closed)		
10. Jumping, feet together		
Comments		

Appendix A - 3

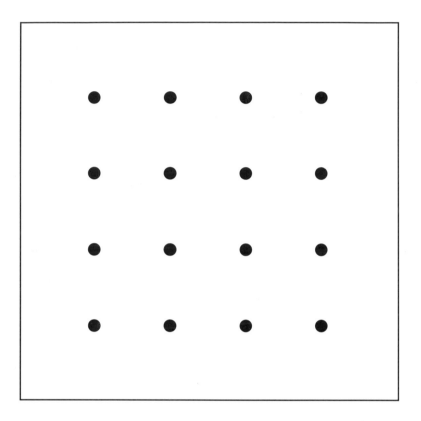

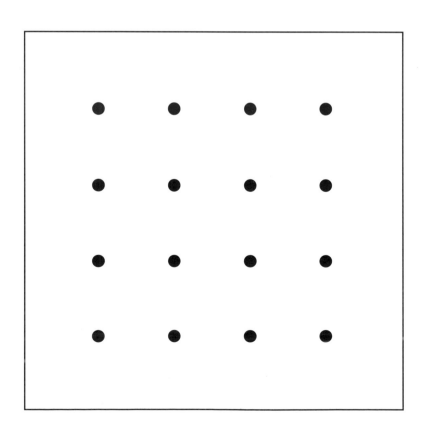

Appendix A - 4

Appendix A - 5

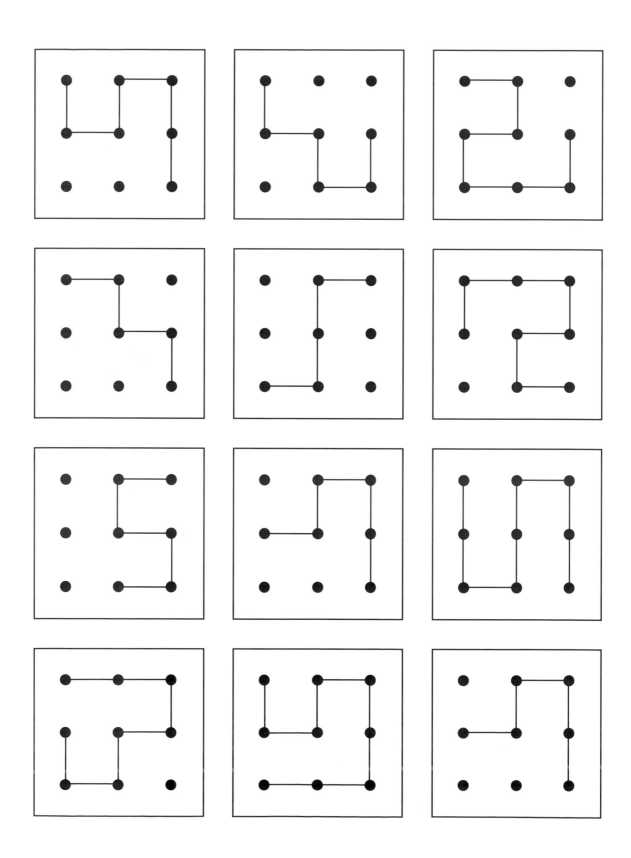

Appendix A - 6

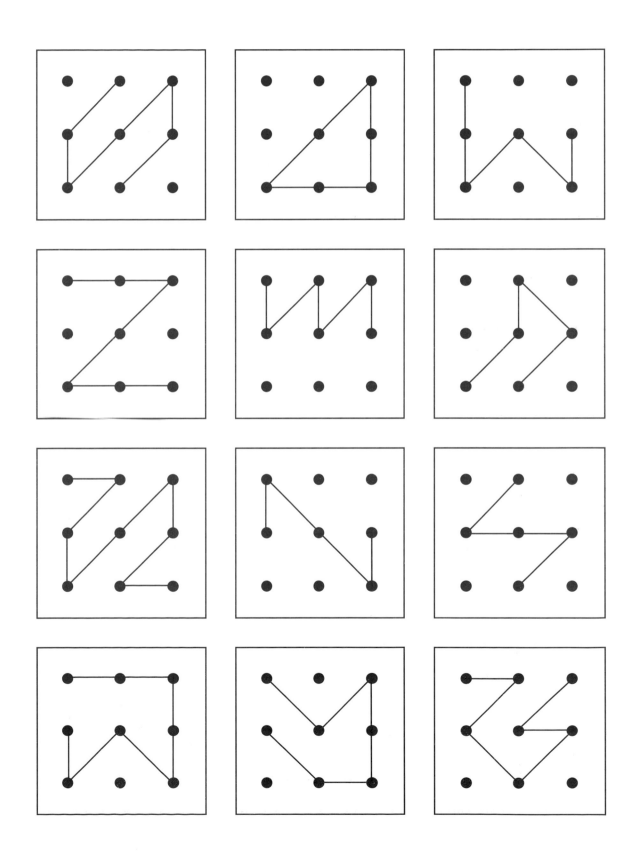

Appendix A - 7

Activity	Mon	Tues	Wed	Thurs	Fri
Comments					

Appendix A - 8

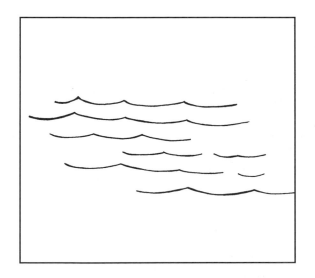

Water play

Sand

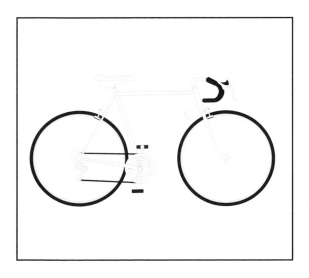

Outdoor activities

Appendix A - 8

Computer

Story-time

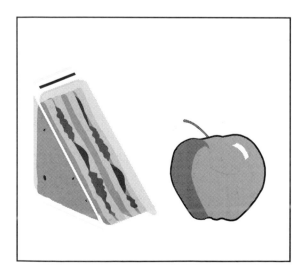

Snack table

Appendix A - 8

Construction

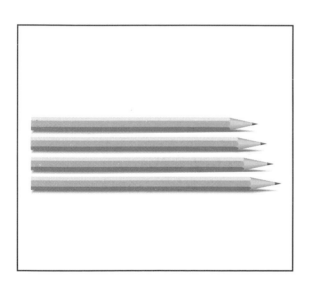

Drawing

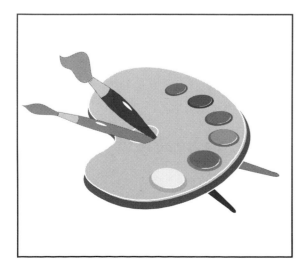

Painting

Appendix A - 8

Home corner

Cloakroom

Co-operative play

Appendix A - 9

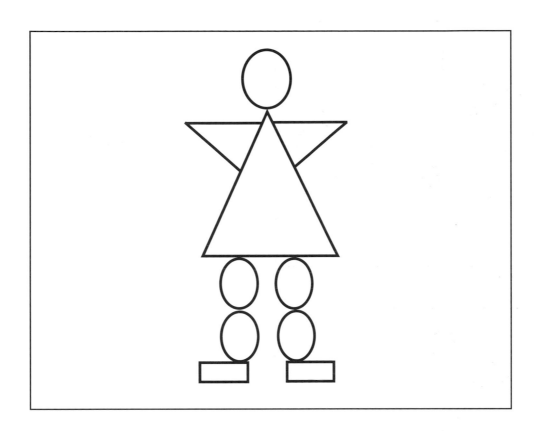

Appendix A - 9

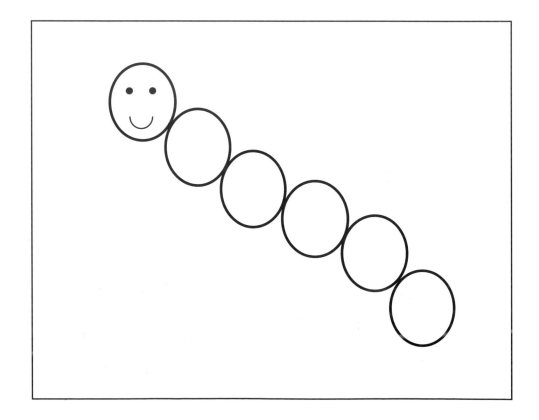

Appendix A - 9

Appendix A - 9

Appendix B

Tumble Tot Licensees

Bill & Jennie Cosgrave
Tumble Tots (UK) Ltd.
Springfield House
2 Millicent Road
Wet Bridgeford
Nottingham
NG2 7LD.

Fax & Telephone number
0115 9815886.

Office Opening Hours
Monday to Thursday
9am - 1pm
Secretary - Wendy Gill

South Area.

Beverley Regan
44 Highview Avenue
Edgeware
Middlesex
HA8 9UA.
0181-9586579

Amanda Stephenson
138 Aylesbury Road
Bierton
Aylesbury
Buckinghamshire
HP22 5DL
01296-394709

Lorraine Harrison
67 Hale Lane
Mill Hill
London
NW7 3PU.
0181-9594261

Anne Kapoor
3 King Edward Road
Barnet
Hertfordshire
EN5 5AW.
0181-4400634

Linda Aspel
Coach House
30A Station Road
Willington
Bedford
MK44 3QH.
01234-838883

Linda Minde
8 Old Hall Close
Hatchend
Pinner
Middlesex
HA5 4ST.
0181-4283462

Lesley Dawson
49 Brackley Road
Westbury
Nr Brackley
Northamptonshire
NN13 5JN.
01280-700766

Beverley Davis
32 South View
Downley
High Wycombe
Buckinghamshire
HP13 5UL
01494-443113

Developmental
— Dyspraxia

Carol Shackell
124 Valley Way
Stevenage
Hertfordshire
SG1 9DD.
01438-369848

Julia Forrest
257 Kent House Road
Beckenham
Kent
BR3 1JQ.
0181-7783830

Ann Young
Little Court,
London Road
Ryarsh West Malling
Kent
ME19 5AH
01732-842497.

Bev Wilkes
164 Whyteleafe Hill
Whyteleafe
Surrey
CR3 OAF.
0181-6601241

Lorraine Puttock
156 Nevill Road
Hove
East Sussex
BN3 7QE.
01273-883782.

Julie Fuller
15 Lyndhurst Road
Hove
East Sussex
BN3 6FA
01273-723511

Veronica Anderson
30 The Suttons
St Leonards on Sea
East Sussex
TN38 9RA.
01424-850265

South West Area.

John and Sue Knight
55 Pepperharow Road
Godalming
Surrey
GU7 2PL.
01483-420741

David Barker/Anne Barrin
68 Brackendale Road
Camberley
Surrey
GU15 2JY
01276-62438

Helen Jutting
46 London Road
Chertsey
Surrey
KT16 8AA
01923-568263

Nicky Bennett
12 Charles Street,
Barnes
London
SW13 ONZ
0181-3929306

Gillian Smith
45 Ottaways Lane
Ashtead
Surrey
KT21 2PS.
01372-273649

Nora Shipley
6 Harkness Close
Epsom Downs
Surrey
KT17 3PG
01737-352375

Nicola Spink
56 Drill Hall Road
Chertsey
Surrey
KT16 8EN
01932-564512

Jane Bayden
29 Silwood
Wooden Hill
Bracknell
Berkshire RG12 8WU.
01344-56492

Carolyn Brown
21 Windsor Street,
Headington
Oxford
OX3 7AP
01865-68443

Jane Beech
124 Childcombe Way,
Lower Earley
Reading
Berkshire
RG6 3DD.
01734-667746

Eastern Area.

Zetha Annan
49 York Hill
Loughton
Essex
IG10 IHZ
0181-5020185

Rosemary Herring
49a Church Road
Wickham Bishops
Essex
CM8 3JZ.
01621-891948

Christine Maidman
Glebe Cottage
Great Saling
Braintree
Essex
CM7 5EW.
01371-850431

Susan Slow
45 Fenwick Way,
Canvey Island
Essex SS9FF
Sue - 01268-699222
Jackie - 01702-559095

Sylvia West
58 School Lane
Toft
Cambridgeshire
CB3 7RE
01223-263412

Jan Smith
Field View
Mill Road
Stokesby
Great Yarmouth,
Norfolk.
NR29 3EY
01493-750520

Conny Wiliamson
118 Second Avenue
Sudbury
Suffolk
CO10 6QY.
01787-373343

Denise Sadler
5 Lancaster Close
Old Catton
Norwich
Norfolk
NR6 7BD.
01683-419074

Western Area

Lorraine Exley
89 Eppleby Road
Parkstone
Poole
Dorset
BH12 3DD
01202-749249

Janet Standley
291 Vigo Road
Andover
Hampshire
SP10 1LA.
01264-353377

Ann Clapham
20 Princes Road
Petersfield
Hampshire
GU32 3BQ
01730-267596

Val and Graham Middle
6 Addicott Road
Weston Super Mare
Avon
BS23 3PX.
01934-417550

Steve Milton
The Fitness Factory
1a Portland Street
Newport
Isle of White
PO30 1QQ
01983-528149

Olive Adams
3/4 Grange Cottages
Barbican
Plympton St Maurice
Plymouth
Devon
PL7 3LU.
01752-347145

Jane Harrisson
19 Barton Close
Exton
Exeter
Devon
EX3 OPE
01392-877515

Combe Grove Manor
Hotel and Country Club
Brassknocker Hill
Monkton Combe
Bath
Avon
BA2 7HS.
01225-835533

North Eastern Area

Clare & Mike Le-Marie
71 The Flatts,
Sowerby
Near Thirsk
North Yorkshire
YO7 1LY.
01845-525977

Sheila Boys
258 Eagle Park
Marton
Middlesbrough
Cleveland
TS8 9QS.
01642-321243

Sue Couture
124 Westend Avenue
Harrogate
North Yorkshire
HG2 9BT.
01423-563731

Anna Linford
The Ashes
5 Church Meadows
Barton
Richmond
North Yorkshire
DL10 6NQ
01325-377576

Maria Barker
Rhodesia House
Northumberland Gardens
North Walbottle
Newcastle upon Tyne
NE5 1PT
0191-2677400

East Midlands.

Irene Jones
The Old Cottage
Scalford Hall
Scalford Road
Melton Mowbray
Leicestershire
LE14 1LB.
01664-444555

Pat Partington
Glen Eden House
Witham on the Hill
Bourne
Lincolnshire
PE10 0JP.
01778-590225

Midlands

Ann Bartram
Glenavon
56 Ashby Road
Tamworth
Staffordshire
B79 8AG.
01827-66318

Linda Hill
2 Captains Lane
Barton under Needwood
Burton on trent
Staffordshire
DE13 8EZ
01283-716499

Helen Priest
Hillview
Oakle Street
Churcham
Glouceshire
GL2 8AG
01452-750242

Denise Padfield
Chapel Farm Cottage
Pratts Lane
Mappleborough Green
Warwickshire
B80 7BW.
01527-857392

Beverley Mills
25 Trinity Close
Solihull
West Midlands
B92 8SZ
0121- 7421503

Developmental
Dyspraxia

Eileen Braham
38 Poplar Road
Bishops Itchington
Warwickshire
CV33 ORQ
01926-614039

Geraldine Pestridge
Brockhurst Park Farm
99 Brockhurst Lane
Canwell
Sutton Coldfield
West Midlands
0121-3080788

Zeeta and John Dowsey
Abernyte Cottage
1st Lukes Road
Ironbridge
Telford
Shropshire
TF8 7PU
01952-433391

North West Area

Martin and Cathy Lawson
24 Darley Road
Hazel Grove
Stockport
Cheshire
SK7 6EA.
O1625-876505

Karen Hickson
'Fair View'
5 Longmoss Close
Middlewich
Cheshire
CW10 OPW.

Liz Edwards
13 Northwards Road
Wilmslow
Cheshire
SK9 6AB.
01625-537602

Sarita Collins
54 Edenfield Road
Rochdale
Lancashire
OL11 5AA.
01706-48128

Sue Livesey
5 Toleman Avenue
Bebington
Wirral
L63 7QA.
0151-6457212

Hilary Bernstein/Simon
48 The Beeches
Druids Cross Road
Liverpool
L18 3LT.
0151-7220618

Cathy Carubia
274 Menlove Avenue
Woolton
Liverpool
L25 6EW
0151-4283710

Clare Rock
11 Redhall Avenue,
Connahs Quay
Deeside
Clwyd
North Wales
01244-822586

Christine Densham
1 Penhill Close
Bexley Gardens
North Shore
Blackpool
FY2 OXP.
01253-355262

Liz Mackenzie
Castlesteads
Burton Road
Oxenholme
LA9 7PR
01539-732613.

Scotland

Karen Dewar
28 Buckstone Circle
Fairmilehead
Edinburgh
EM10 6XQ
0131-4451464

Paula Tatters
Fitness & Fun
130 High Street
Elgin
Morayshire
Scotland
IV30 1BW.
01343-549307

Jan Martin
Lea Park
Perth Road
Blairgowrie
PH10 6EQ
01250-874561

Jan Martin
Fairlawn
1 Ralston Road
Bearsden
Glasgow
G61 3SS
0141-9422790

Jo Letelier-Lobos
Templehall Farm
Puddledub
Auchtestoo
Fife
KY2 5XA.
01592-873287

Ireland

Claire and James Ogg
Hogstown House
Hogstown Road
Donaghadee
County Down
Northern Ireland
BT21 ONL.
01247-888432

Lynne Stewart
49 Ballymacash Road
Lisburn
County Antrim
Northern Ireland
BT28 3ER.
01846-666146

Appendix C

Equipment and the names and addresses of suppliers

Ayres Collection for Development (A.C.)
Ayres and Co. Ltd.
Unit 1
Turnoaks Business Park
Burley Close
Chesterfield
S40 2HA   *Tel: 01246 551546*

Early Learning Centre (E.L.C.)
South Marston Park
Swindon
SN3 4TJ   *Tel: 01793 444844*

Galt Education (G.E.)
Culvert Street
Oldham
Lancashire
OL4 2ST   *Tel: 0161 6275086*

Mr. J. Jacob
Howden-Le-Wear Primary School
Howden-le-Wear
Bishop Auckland
Co. Durham   *Tel: 01388 763287*

Mr. A. Potts
Howden-le-Wear
Bishop Auckland
Co. Durham   *Tel: 01388 763350*

N.E.S. Arnold Ltd. (N.E.S.)
Ludlow Hill Road
West Bridgford
Nottingham
NG2 6HD   *Tel: 0115 9452201*

Tumble Tots Equipment (T.T.)
Blue Bird Park
Bromsgrove Road
Hunnington
Halesowen
West Midlands
B62 OJW   *Tel: 0121 5857003*

Actipack - practical activities to develop mathematical skills with 8-13 year olds.
N.E.S.

Adjustable wobble boards - wooden base screw attachment for adjustable height.
J. Jacob

Assorted form balls - lightweight, varying sizes and colours.
N.E.S. E.L.C.

Basket ball net - forms an early introduction to ball skills. Adjustable height - ball included.
G.E.

Bean bags - set of 12 in assorted colours.
G.E. T.T.

Chime bars - 8 coloured chimes which can be removed from tray. Comes with 3 pairs of hammers.
N.E.S. G.E.

Climbing frame - wooden hardwood frame with two platforms of variable height.
N.E.S. C.E.

Creepies - crawlie puppets - hand puppets designed to make the fingers appear to form the legs of the insets. 2 sizes adult and child. Finger puppets are also available.
G.E.

Cutting fruit - apple, pear and lemon. Pieces attached with Velcro. Comes with a wooden knife.
G.E.

Cutting vegetables - 11 different fruits and vegetables attached with velcro. Special plastic knife provided.
E.L.C.

Desk music stands - inexpensive plastic stands which will hold reading material in an angled position.
N.E.S.

Diagnostic development frames - progressively extends eye-hand co-ordination which is essential for the development of a range of physical and intellectual skills. See 'training aids'.
N.E.S.

Dot to dot pictures - simple pictures for young children to develop pencil control skills. Maximum of 20 dots.
E.L.C.

Easel -	adjustable drawing easel, various attachments. G.E. E.L.C.
Easihold rulers -	designed to enable the child with poor co-ordination to hold ruler more securely. Flat surface with handle attachment. A. Potts
Finger Puppets -	12 characters from nursery rhymes children story finger puppets. N.E.S.
Foam dart board -	velcro tipped darts and colourful felt target, encourages number skills and eye-hand co-ordination. E.L.C.
Foam fishing -	fun game to play in the bath, develops eye-hand co-ordination. E.L.C.
Geo nuts and bolts -	a set of giant nuts and bolts which can be twisted together. Matched for shape and colour. Designed for small fingers to gain dexterity. N.E.S.
Geo-board -	a sorting board with 4 different shapes. N.E.S.
Geometrix -	a 2 dimensional game based on colour, shape and farm matching. Patterns progress from very simple shapes to more complex abstract figures. N.E.S.
Gym Equipment under 7's -	slide, ladders, stepping stones, balancing beams, meccano walkway. N.E.S., T.T., G.E
Hand and foot-prints -	provide a directional pathway for movement giving the child cues for placing feet and hands. N.E.S.
Hand looms -	2 sizes small - nursery reception class, large 6+. A. Potts
Happy matrix -	3 different themes. Each pack contains 5 sets of illustrated coloured cards, a laminated matrix board and computer software which enables the game to be played on the table top or on the computer screen. A.L.

Hedgehog balls -	for massage, hand and finger exercises or for throwing and catching. Available in 3 sizes. A.C.
Hoops -	assorted colours and sizes. G.E.
Inset boards -	large handled, fruit, everyday objects. N.E.S., G.E., A.L.
Lacing fruit -	large holes allow the big wooden threader to pass through. Ideal for developing basic co-ordination skills. N.E.S.
Letter shapes -	26 boards, one for each letter incorporating a series of graded letter grooves. As the letter sizes decrease children gradually acquire more controlled motor skills to help them form the letters correctly. N.E.S.
Logic materials -	sorting activities and introduction of logic. Comprises assortment of plastic pieces with P.V.C. templates. N.E.S.
Magnetic fish game -	suitable from 3+. Designed to develop hand and eye co-ordination. N.E.S.
Magnetic playdesk -	magnetic angled board with 37 numbers, 40 upper and 40 lower case letters. E.L.C.
Magnetic shapes -	Piky decors and mosaic. Magnetised pieces in various shapes and sizes. Develops understanding of shape. N.E.S.
Math safari -	highly motivating scheme to teach mathematics from age 4. Pupils can use it individually or play competitively. Angled board for easy viewing. Scheme reduced the amount of hand-written recording. N.E.S.
Mega blocks -	large bright building blocks which develop co-ordination skills. G.E. Woolworths.

Mini hurdles -	4 hardwood hurdles - height 11.5 c.m. G.E.
Moulding day and Play Doh -	modelling material that is east to manipulate. Assorted colour. G.E.
Mounted chime bars. -	development of rhythm and extension of hand movements. A.C.
Multi-link -	fractions, exploring angles and algebra through structures. Suitable for youngsters aged 7-11. Develops understanding of mathematical concepts with emphasis on practical activities. N.E.S.
Multi-link pattern cards -	3 sets of pattern cards designed to be placed on the multi-link grid tray under the transparent grid. Cubes may then be put down onto the grid to match the pattern underneath. Develop skills in colour matching, making patterns, language development and they extend a child's perceptual skills and recording ability. N.E.S.
Pedal - go - wheeled activity -	designed to improve balance, co-ordination and motor control skills. G.E.
Pegboards -	boards and pegs are available in different sizes. Designed to improve eye-hand co-ordination. G.E.
Picture lotto -	6 wooden boards with 54 matching pieces. Designed to encourage language development. N.E.S.
Play Tunnel -	heavy duty reinforced plastic. N.E.S. E.L.C.
Pre-writing -	2 wooden panels with cut out tracks of different degrees of difficulty. The aim is to pull the bead/knob along the pre-determined track. Develops pre-writing skills and assists with eye-hand co-ordination. A.L.
Pre-writing skills worksheets -	30 re-usable worksheets which provide a series of finely graded exercises to encourage left-to-right tracking skills and basic letter patterns. N.E.S.

Reward chart -	laminated write on/wipe off surface, records activities on a weekly basis. Includes pens, stars and reward coupons. T.T.
Rol 'n' Write -	a steel ball slowly traces the letter in the correct sequence. Alternatively the children can follow the grove with their fingers. In addition there are 48 photocopy masters to complete. Develops fine motor control, hand-eye co-ordination, fluency and flow of hand and letter formation. N.E.S.
Sand shapers -	5 differently shapes moulds. G.E.
Self opening scissors -	designed for small hands or children with a weak grip. They allow the strength in all the fingers to used when cutting. A spring is incorporated into the handles to pull open the blades. G.E.
SENSO -	a lotto game which focuses on the development of tactile skills as well as stimulating visual language and simple country skills. N.E.S.
Sequencing colour cards -	12, 4 step sequences. Easy to understand concepts in familiar domestic scenes. A.C.
Sequential colour cards -	12, 4 step sequences. Easy to understand concepts in familiar domestic scenes. A.L.
Sequential thinking cards -	each sequence shows familiar situations such as getting ready for bed, crossing the road etc. Through sets 1-5 the sequences become visually and logically more complex. Stimulates imagination and language development. Set 1 3 x 2 card, 4 x 3 card, 3 x 4 card sequences. A.C.
Short tennis racquets -	large surface heads and short handles. Ideal for youngsters learning to co-ordinate movements between bat and ball. N.E.S.
Stampabouts -	improves balance, cords held taut while feet are lifted. N.E.S.

Star - stack -	available in 2 sizes, 6 pronged shapes fit together to form increasingly complex structures. N.E.S.
Stirex scissors -	designed to help children who have a weaker grip. Operated using the whole hand rather than the forefinger and thumb. G.E.
Tactile letters -	letter template and soft shiny colourful p.v.c letters. Extends language. G.E.
Tactile touch cards -	34 cards to demonstrate a range of different tactile sensations such as smooth and rough, thick and thin. G.E.
Targets -	wooden design 50 c.m.^{2} Inner target 15 c.m. chain, outer target 35 c.m. diameter. M.
Threading butterfly -	easy to thread shape. A.L.
Training aids -	designed specifically to develop perceptual, motor, manipulative and language skills. Blocks are manoeuvred around a wire frame and it is a test of eye-hand co-ordination. A precursor to writing skills. G.E.
Training scissors -	double handed to teach youngster with poor motor skills. G.E.
Trampoline -	steel frame complete with handrail. Suitable for 2 years +. N.E.S. E.L.C.
Triangular pencils -	chunky pencils designed to help children develop drawing and writing skills. The grip gives better control improved comfort and less writing fatigue.
Waffle blocks -	36 blocks in assorted colours. Easy to manipulate. G.E.

Dyspraxia Trust	P.O. Box 30 Hitchin Herts SG5 1UU

*R*eferences

Bruininks, R.H., (1978) *Bruininks - Oseretsky test of motor proficiency.*
Circle Pines, American Guidance Service.

Caramazza. A., Gordon, J., Zurif, E.N., & DeLuca, Da. (1976).
Right-hemispheric damage and verbal problem solving
behaviour. *Brain and Language, 3*, 41-46.

Carramazza, A., (1986). On drawing inferences about the structure of
normal cognitive systems from the analysis of patterns of impaired
performance: The case for single-patient studies.
Brain and Cognition, 5, 41-66.

Code, C., (1987). *Language, aphasia and the right hemisphere.*
Chichester: John Wiley.

Coltheart, M., (1983). The right hemisphere and disorders of reading. In
A.W. Young (Ed.), *Functions of the right cerebral hemisphere.*
London: Academic Press.

Damasio, A. R. & Benton, A. L. (1979). Impairment of hand
movements under visual guidance. *Neurology, 29* 170-178.

Edelman, G.M., (1989). Neural Darwinism. *The theory of neuronal
group selection.* Oxford University Press.

Edelman, G.M., (1992). *Brilliant fire on the matter of the mind.* A.
Lane Pubs.

Edwards, B., (1979) *Drawing on the right side of the brain.* Tarcher,
Los Angeles.

Ellis, A. W., (1983). Syndromes, slips and structures. *Bulletin of the
British Psychological Society, 36,* 372-374.

Ellis, A. W., (1987). Intimations of modularity, or, The modularity of
mind. In M. Coltheart, G, Sartoria, & R. Job (Eds), *The cognitive
neuropsychology of language.* London: Lawrence Erlbaum
Associates Ltd.

Ellis, A. W., (1982). Spelling and writing (and reading and speaking).
In A.W. Ellis (Ed.), *Normality and pathology in cognitive functions.*
London: Academic Press.

Ellis, A., & Young, A., (1988). *Human cognitive neuropsychology.*
Lawrence Erlbaum Associates, Hillsdale (USA).

Frith, U., (Ed.) (1980). *Cognitive processes in spelling.* London:
Academic Press.

Frostig, M. *Developmental Test of Visual Perception.* Consulting Psychological Press, California.

Goodman, R. A., & Caramazza, A. (1986c). Aspects of the spelling process: Evidence from a case of acquired dysgraphia. *Language and Cognitive Processes, 1,* 1-34.

Griffiths, R., *Griffiths Mental Development Scales.* Test Agency, High Wycombe.

Gubbay, S.S., (1985) Clumsiness. In Vinken P. Bruyn G. & Dlawans H. *Handbook of Clinical Neurology.* New York. Elsevier.

Hécaen, H. & Marcie, P. (1974). Disorders of written language following right hemisphere lesions. In S. J. Dimond & J. G. Beaumont (Eds), *Hemisphere function in the human brain.* London: Elek.

Henderson, S. & Sugden, D. (1992) *Movement assessment battery for children.* The Psychological Corporation.

Hier, D. B. & Kaplan, J., (1980). Verbal comprehension deficits after right hemisphere damage. *Applied Psycholinguistics, I,* 279-294.

Hotopf, W. H. N., (1980). Slips of the pen. In U. Frith (Ed.), *Cognitive processes in spelling.* London: Academic Press.

Keller, E. & Gopnik., M. (Eds) (1987). *Motor and sensory processes of language.* Hillsdale, N. J.: Lawrence Erlbaum Associates.

Kimura, D. & Archibald, Y. (1974). Motor functions of the left hemisphere. *Brain, 97,* 333-350.

Luria, A. R. (1976). *Basic problems in neurolinguistics.* The Hague: Mouton.

Margolin, D. I. (1984). The neuropsychology of writing and spelling: Semantic, phonological, motor and perceptual processes. *Quarterly Journal of Experimental Psychology, 36A,* 459-489.

Miceli, G., Silveri, C., & Caramazza, A. (1985). Cognitive analysis of a case of pure dysgraphia. *Brain and Language, 26,* 187-212.

Patterson, K. & Kay, J. (1982). Letter-by-letter reading: Psychological descriptions of a neurological syndrome. *Quarterly Journal of Experimental Psychology, 34A,* 411-441.

Patterson, K. E. & Besner, D. (1984). Is the right hemisphere literate? *Cognitive Neuropsychology, 1,* 315-341.

Posner, M. I., Cohen, Y., & Rafal, R. D. (1982). Neural systems control of spatial orienting. *Philosophical Transactions of the Royal Society* (London), B298, 187-198.

Posner, M. I., Rafal, R. D., Choate, L. S., & Vaughan, J. (1985). Inhibition of return: Neural basis and function. *Cognitive Neuropsychology, 2,* 211-228.

Russell, J., (1988). *Graded activities for children with motor difficulties.* Cambridge University Press.

Saffran, E. M., (1982). Neuropsychological approaches to the study of language. *British Journal of Psychology, 73,* 317-337.

Sandler, A. Watson, T., Footo M., et al. (1992). Neurodevelopmental study of writing disorders in middle childhood. *Journal of Developmental and Behavioural Paediatrics;* 13:17-23.

Searleman, A., (1983). Language capabilities of the right hemisphere. In A.W. Young (Ed.), *Functions of the right cerebral hemisphere,* London: Academic Press.

Shaley, R., Manar, O., Amir N., Gross-Tsur, V., (1993). The acquisition of arithmetic in normal children: Assessment by a cognitive model of dyscalculia. *Developmental Medicine and Child Neurology.* 35:539-601.

Shalice, T., (1981a). Neurological impairment of cognitive processes. *British Medical Bulletin, 37,* 187-192.

Van Galen, G. P., (1980). Handwriting and drawing: A two-stage model of complex motor behaviour.

Wechsler, D., WPPSI - R.UK., WISC - III, WAIS, The Psychological Corporation.

White, M., Bungay, C., & Gabriel, H., (1994) *Guide to early movement skills.* NFER-Nelson.

Williams, L.V., (1983). *Teaching for the two-sided mind.* Simon & Schuster Inc. New York.